ETIQUETTE

AND THE

LANGUAGE OF FLOWERS

1883

This book is a partial reprint of Collier's *Cyclopedia of Social and Commercial Information*, published in 1883. New material and edited content are © C. S. Friedman.

Special thanks to Kim Dobson, whose generosity of spirit made this project possible.

ISBN: 978-1-737-1619-8-1

TRIDAC
PUBLISHING

INTRODUCTION

IF EVER an Age of Etiquette existed, the nineteenth century was it. Virtually every aspect of life was governed by a code of proper behavior, and those who wished to be well-regarded by their peers—and hopefully their betters—had to follow it. There were different rules for men and women, both for their own behavior and the manner in which others approached them, and anyone hoping to move up the social ladder needed to respect those distinctions. A few mavericks did defy the system, earning respect through notoriety rather than conformity, but such cases were few and far between. For most, proper etiquette was a prerequisite for social advancement.

But why such a fixation upon rules? The *Laws of Etiquette*, published in 1837, suggested that the code of etiquette served to maintain class distinctions, and that Americans were even more obsessed with etiquette than their British cousins.

> *There is perfect freedom of political privilege, all are the same upon the hustings, or at a political meeting; but this equality does not extend to the drawing room. None are excluded from the highest councils of the nation, but it does not follow that all can enter into the highest ranks of society. In point of fact, we think that there is more exclusiveness in the society of this country, than there is in that even of England—far more than there is in France. There being there less danger of permanent disarrangement or confusion of ranks by the occasional admission of the low-born aspirant, there does not exist the same necessity for a jealous guarding of barriers as there does here.*

One of the most exhaustive lists of etiquette instructions was published in *Collier's 1883 Cyclopedia of Social and Commercial Information.* With over 50 pages of rules for every aspect of social activity, as well as fashion advice and instructions for popular dances, it provides the modern reader with a window into nineteenth-century society, and sheds light upon the evolution of gender roles. It is my pleasure to offer it here in its original form, complete with lavish Victorian embellishments.

Celia S. Friedman
Sterling, Virginia

ETIQUETTE FOR LADIES.

ETIQUETTE may be defined as the minor morality of life. Its laws, like all other social laws, are the accumulated results of the wisdom and experience of many generations. They form a code with which every educated person is bound to be acquainted; and the object of this portion of Collier's Cyclopedia is to place that code before the reader in as succinct, as agreeable, and as explanatory a light as the subject admits of. We hope and believe that it will be found in all respects a trusty and pleasant guide.

INTRODUCTIONS.

To introduce persons who are mutually unknown is to undertake a serious responsibility, and to certify to each the respectability of the other. Never undertake this responsibility without, in the first place, asking yourself whether the persons are likely to be agreeable to each other; nor, in the second place, without ascertaining whether it will be acceptable to both parties to become acquainted.

Always introduce the gentleman to the lady—never the lady to the gentleman. The chivalry of etiquette assumes that the lady is invariably the superior in right of her sex, and that the gentleman is honored in the introduction.

Never present a gentleman to a lady without first asking her permission to do so.

When you are introduced to a gentleman, never offer your hand. When introduced, persons limit their recognition of each other to a bow.

Persons who have met at the house of a mutual friend without being introduced should not bow if they afterwards meet elsewhere. A bow implies acquaintance; and persons who have not been introduced are not acquainted.

If you are walking with one friend, and presently meet with, or are joined by, a second, do not commit the too frequent error of introducing them to each other. You have even less right to do so than if they encountered each other at your house during a morning call.

There are some exceptions to the etiquette of introduction. At a ball, or evening party where there is dancing, the mistress of the house may introduce any gentleman to any lady without first asking the lady's permission. But she should first ascertain whether the lady is willing to dance; and this out of consideration for the gentleman, who may otherwise be refused. No man likes to be refused the hand of a lady, though it be only for a quadrille.

A sister may present her brother, or a mother her son, without any kind of preliminary.

Friends may introduce friends at the house of a mutual acquaintance; but, as a rule, it is better to be introduced by the mistress of the house. Such an introduction carries more authority with it.

Introductions at evening parties are now almost wholly dispensed with. Persons who meet at a friend's house are ostensibly upon an equality, and pay a bad compliment to the host by appearing suspicious and formal. Some old-fashioned country hosts still persevere in introducing each new comer to all the assembled guests. It is a custom that cannot be too soon abolished, and one that places the last unfortunate visitor in a singularly awkward position. All that she can do is to make a semicircular courtesy, like a concert singer before an audience, and bear the general gaze with as much composure as possible.

An introduction given at a ball for the mere purpose of conducting a lady through a dance does not give the gentleman any right to bow to her on a future occasion. If he commits this error, she may remember that she is not bound to see, or return, his salutation.

LETTERS OF INTRODUCTION.

Do not lightly give or promise letters of introduction. Always remember that when you give a letter of introduction you lay yourself under an obligation to the friend to whom it is addressed. If she lives in a great city, such as Chicago or Boston, you in a measure compel her to undergo the penalty of escorting the stranger to some of those places of public entertainment in which the capital abounds. If your friend be a married lady, and the mistress of a house, you put her to the expense of inviting the stranger to her table. We cannot be too cautious how we tax the time and purse of a friend, or weigh too seriously the question of mutual advantage in the introduction. Always ask yourself whether the person introduced will be an acceptable acquaintance to the one to whom you present her; and whether the pleasure of knowing her will compensate for the time or money which it costs to entertain her. If the stranger is in any way unsuitable in habits or temperament, you inflict an annoyance on your friend instead of a pleasure. In questions of introduction never oblige one friend to the discomfort of another.

Those to whom letters of introduction have been given should send them to the person to whom they are addressed, and inclose a card. Avoid delivering a letter of introduction in person. It places you in the most undignified position imaginable, and compels you to wait while it is being read, like a servant who has been told to wait for an answer. If the receiver of the letter be a really well-bred person, she will call upon you or leave her card the next day, and you should return her attention within the week.

If, on the other hand, a stranger sends you a letter of introduction and her card, you are bound by the laws of politeness and hospitality, not only to call upon her the next day, but to follow up that attention with others. If you are in a position to do so, the most correct proceeding is to invite her to dine with you. Should this not be within your power, you can probably escort her to some of the exhibitions, bazaars, or concerts of the season; any of which would be interesting to a provincial visitor. In short, etiquette demands that you shall exert yourself to show kindness to the stranger, if only out of compliment to the friend who introduced her to you.

If you invite her to take dinner with you, it is a better compliment to ask some others to meet her than to dine with her *tête-à-tête*. You are thereby giving her an opportunity of making other acquaintances, and are assisting your friend in still farther promoting the purpose for which she gave her the introduction to yourself.

A letter of introduction should be given unsealed, not alone because your friend may wish to know what you have said of her, but also as a guarantee of your own good faith. As you should never give such a letter unless you can speak highly of the bearer, this rule of etiquette is easy to observe. By requesting your friend to fasten the envelope before forwarding the letter to its destination, you tacitly give her permission to inspect its contents.

VISITING CARDS.

Visits of ceremony should be short. If even the conversation should have become animated, beware of letting your call exceed half-an-hour's length. It is always better to let your friends regret rather than desire your withdrawal.

On returning visits of ceremony you may, without impoliteness, leave your card at the door without going in. Do not fail, however, to inquire if the family be well.

Should there be daughters or sisters residing with the lady upon whom you call, you may turn down a corner of your card, to signify that the visit is paid to all. It is in better taste, however, to leave cards for each.

Unless when returning thanks for "kind inquiries," or announcing your arrival in, or departure from, town, it is not considered respectful to send round cards by a servant.

Leave-taking cards have P.P.C. (*pour prendre congé*) written in the corner. Some use P.D.A. (*pour dire adieu*).

Autographic facsimiles for visiting cards are affectations in any persons but those who are personally remarkable for talent, and whose autographs, or facsimiles of them, would be prized as curiosities.

Visits of condolence are paid within the week after the event which occasions them. Personal visits of this kind are made by relations and very intimate friends only. Acquaintances should leave cards with narrow mourning borders.

On the first occasion when you are received by the family after the death of one of its members, it is etiquette to wear slight mourning.

Umbrellas should invariably be left in the hall.

Never take favorite dogs into a drawing-room when you make a morning call. Their feet may be dusty, or they may bark at the sight of strangers, or, being of a too friendly disposition, may take the liberty of lying on a lady's gown, or jumping on the sofas and easy chairs. Where your friend has a favorite cat already established before the fire, a battle may ensue, and one or both of the pets be seriously hurt. Besides, many persons have a constitutional antipathy to dogs, and others never allow their own to be seen in the sitting-rooms. For all or any of these reasons, a visitor has no right to inflict upon her friend the society of her dog as well as of herself. Neither is it well for a mother to take young children with her when she pays morning visits; their presence, unless they are unusually well trained, can only be productive of anxiety to both yourself and your hostess. She, while striving to amuse them, or to appear interested in them, is secretly anxious for the fate of her album, or the ornaments on her *étagère*; while the mother is trembling lest her children should say or do something objectionable.

If other visitors are announced, and you have already remained as long as courtesy requires, wait till they are seated, and then rise from your chair, take leave of your hostess, and bow politely to the newly arrived guests. You will, perhaps, be urged to remain, but, having once risen, it is best to go. There is always a certain air of *gaucherie* in resuming your seat and repeating the ceremony of leave-taking.

If you have occasion to look at your watch during a call, ask permission to do so, and apologize for it on the plea of other appointments.

In receiving morning visitors, it is not necessary that the lady should lay aside the employment in which she may be engaged, particularly if it consists of light or ornamental needle-work.

Politeness, however, requires that music, drawing, or any occupation which would completely engross the attention, be at once abandoned.

You need not advance to receive visitors when announced, unless they are persons to whom you are desirous of testifying particular attention. It is sufficient if a lady rises to receive her visitors, moves forward a single step to shake hands with them, and remains standing till they are seated.

When your visitors rise to take leave you should rise also, and remain standing till they have quite left the room.

A lady should dress well, but not too richly, when she pays a morning visit.

CONVERSATION.

There is no conversation so graceful, so varied, so sparkling, as that of an intellectual and cultivated woman. Excellence in this particular is, indeed, one of the attributes of the sex, and should be cultivated by every gentlewoman who aspires to please in general society.

In order to talk well, three conditions are indispensable, namely—tact, a good memory, and a fair education.

Remember that people take more interest in their own affairs than in anything else which you can name. If you wish your conversation to be thoroughly agreeable, lead a mother to talk of her children, a young lady of her last ball, an author of his forthcoming book, or an artist of his exhibition picture. Having furnished the topic, you need only listen; and you are sure to be thought not only agreeable, but thoroughly sensible and well-informed.

Be careful, however, on the other hand, not always to make a point of talking to persons upon general matters relating to their profession. To show an interest in their immediate concerns is flattering; but to converse with them too much about their own arts looks as if you thought them ignorant of other topics.

Remember in conversation that a voice "gentle and low" is, above all other extraneous acquirements, "an excellent thing in woman." There is a certain distinct but subdued tone of voice which is peculiar to only well-bred persons. A loud voice is both disagreeable and vulgar. It is better to err by the use of too low rather than too loud a tone.

Remember that all "slang" is vulgar.

The use of proverbs is equally vulgar in conversation; and puns, unless they rise to the rank of witticisms, are to be scrupulously avoided. A lady-punster is a most unpleasing phenomenon, and we would advise no young woman, however witty she may be, to cultivate this kind of verbal talent.

Long arguments in general company, however entertaining to the disputants, are tiresome to the last degree to all others. You should always endeavor to prevent the conversation from dwelling too long upon one topic.

Religion is a topic which should never be introduced into society. It is the one subject on which persons are most likely to differ, and least able to preserve temper.

Never interrupt a person who is speaking. It has been aptly said that "if you interrupt a speaker in the middle of his sentence, you act almost as rudely as if, when walking with a companion, you were to thrust yourself before him, and stop his progress."

To listen well is almost as great an art as to talk well. It is not enough *only* to listen. You must endeavor to seem interested in the conversation of others.

It is considered extremely ill bred when two persons whisper in society, or converse in a language with which all present are not familiar. If you have private matters to discuss, you should appoint a proper time and place to do so, without paying others the ill compliment of excluding them from your conversation.

If a foreigner be one of the guests at a small party, and does not understand English sufficiently to follow what is said, good breeding demands that the conversation shall be carried on in his own language. If at a dinner-party, the same rule applies to those at his end of the table.

If upon the entrance of a visitor you carry on the thread of a previous conversation, you should briefly recapitulate to him what has been said before he arrived.

Do not be *always* witty, even though you should be so happily gifted as to need the caution. To outshine others on every occasion is the surest road to unpopularity.

Always look, but never stare, at those with whom you converse.

In order to meet the general needs of conversation in society, it is necessary that a gentlewoman should be acquainted with the current news and historical events of, at least, the last few years.

Never talk upon subjects of which you know nothing, unless it be for the purpose of acquiring information. Many young ladies imagine that because they play a little, sing a little, draw a little, and frequent exhibitions and operas, they are qualified judges of art. No mistake is more egregious or universal.

Those who introduce anecdotes into their conversation are warned that these should invariably be "short, witty, eloquent, new, and not far-fetched."

Scandal is the least excusable of all conversational vulgarities.

DRESS.

To dress well requires something more than a full purse and a pretty figure. It needs taste, good sense, and refinement. Dress may almost be classed as one of the fine arts. It is certainly one of those arts the cultivation of which is indispensable to any person moving in the upper or middle classes of society. Very clever women are too frequently indifferent to the graces of the toilette; and women who wish to be thought clever affect indifference. In the one case it is an error, and in the other a folly. It is not enough that a gentlewoman should be clever, or well educated, or well-born. To take her due place in society, she must be acquainted with all that this little book proposes to teach. She must, above all else, know how to enter a room, how to perform a graceful salutation, and how to dress. Of these three important qualifications, the most important, because the most observed, is the latter.

Let your style of dress always be appropriate to the hour of the day. To dress too finely in the morning, or to be seen in a morning dress in the evening, is equally vulgar and out of place.

Light and inexpensive materials are fittest for morning wear; dark silk dresses for the promenade or carriage; and low dresses of rich or transparent stuffs for the dinner and ball. A young lady cannot dress with too much simplicity in the early part of the day. A morning dress of some simple material, and delicate whole color, with collar and cuffs of spotless linen, is, perhaps, the most becoming and elegant of morning toilettes.

Never dress very richly or showily in the street. It attracts attention of no enviable kind, and is looked upon as a want of good breeding. In the carriage a lady may dress as elegantly as she pleases. With respect to ball-room toilette, its fashions are so variable, that statements which are true of it to-day may be false a month hence. Respecting no institution of modern society, is it so difficult to pronounce half-a-dozen permanent rules.

We may, perhaps, be permitted to suggest the following leading principles; but we do so with diffidence. Rich colors harmonize with rich brunette complexions and dark hair. Delicate colors are the most suitable for delicate and fragile styles of beauty. Very young ladies are never so suitably attired as in white. Ladies who dance should wear dresses of light and diaphanous materials, such as *tulle*, gauze, crape, net, etc., over colored silk slips. Silk dresses are not suitable for dancing. A married lady who dances only a few quadrilles may wear a *décolleté* silk dress with propriety.

Very stout persons should never wear white. It has the effect of adding to the bulk of the figure.

Black and scarlet, or black and violet, are worn in mourning.

A lady in deep mourning should not dance at all.

However fashionable it may be to wear very long dresses, those ladies who go to a ball with the intention of dancing, and enjoying the dance, should cause their dresses to be made short enough to clear the ground. We would ask them whether it is not better to accept this slight deviation from an absurd fashion, than to appear for three parts of the evening in a torn and pinned-up skirt?

Well-made shoes, whatever their color or material, and faultless gloves, are indispensable to the effect of a ball-room toilette.

Much jewelry is out of place in a ball-room. Beautiful flowers, whether natural or artificial, are the loveliest ornaments that a lady can wear on these occasions.

At small dinner parties, low dresses are not so indispensable as they were held to be some years since. High dresses of transparent materials, and low bodices with capes of black lace, are considered sufficiently full dress on these occasions. At large dinners only the fullest dress is appropriate.

Very young ladies should wear but little jewelry. Pearls are deemed most appropriate for the young and unmarried.

Let your jewelry be always the best of its kind. Nothing is so vulgar, either in youth or in age, as the use of false ornaments.

There is as much propriety to be observed in the wearing of jewelry as in the wearing of dresses. Diamonds, pearls, rubies, and all transparent precious stones, belong to evening dress, and should on no account be worn before dinner. In the morning let your rings be of the more simple and massive kind; wear no bracelets; and limit your jewelry to a good brooch, gold chain, and watch. Your diamonds and pearls would be as much out of place during the morning as a low dress, or a wreath.

It is well to remember in the choice of jewelry that mere costliness is not always the test of value; and that an exquisite work of art, such as a fine cameo, or a natural rarity, such as black pearl, is a more *distingué* possession than a large brilliant which any rich and tasteless vulgarian can buy as easily as yourself. Of all precious stones, the opal is one of the most lovely and least common-place. No vulgar woman purchases an opal. She invariably prefers the more showy ruby, emerald, or sapphire.

A true gentlewoman is always faultlessly neat. No richness of toilette in the afternoon, no diamonds in the evening, can atone for unbrushed hair, a soiled collar, or untidy slippers at breakfast.

Never be seen in the street without gloves. Your gloves should fit to the last degree of perfection.

In these days of public baths and universal progress, we trust that it is unnecessary to do more than hint at the necessity of the most fastidious personal cleanliness. The hair, the teeth, the nails, should be faultlessly kept; and a muslin dress that has been worn once too often, a dingy pocket-handkerchief, or a soiled pair of light gloves, are things to be scrupulously avoided by any young lady who is ambitious of preserving the exterior of a gentlewoman.

Remember that the make of your *corsage* is of even greater importance than the make of your dress. No dressmaker can fit you well, or make your bodices in the manner most becoming to your figure, if the *corsage* beneath be not of the best description.

Your shoes and gloves should always be faultless.

Perfumes should be used only in the evening, and then in moderation. Let your perfumes be of the most delicate and *recherché* kind. Nothing is more vulgar than a coarse, ordinary scent; and of all coarse, ordinary scents, the most objectionable are musk and patchouli.

Finally, every lady should remember that to dress well is a duty which she owes to society; but that to make it her idol is to commit something worse than a folly. Fashion is made for woman; not woman for fashion.

MORNING AND EVENING PARTIES.

The morning party is a modern invention. It was unknown to our fathers and mothers, and even to ourselves till quite lately. A morning party is given during the months of June, July, August, September, and sometimes October. It begins about two o'clock and ends about seven, and the entertainment consists for the most part of conversation, music, and (if there be a garden) croquet, lawn tennis, archery, etc. The refreshments are given in the form of a *déjeûner à la fourchette*. Receptions are held during the winter season.

Elegant morning dress, general good manners, and some acquaintance with the topics of the day and the games above named, are all the qualifications especially necessary to a lady at a morning party, and "At Homes;" music and elocution at receptions.

An evening party begins about nine o'clock p.m., and ends about midnight, or somewhat later. Good-breeding neither demands that you should present yourself at the commencement, nor remain till the close of the evening. You come and go as may be most convenient to you, and by these means are at liberty, during the height of the season when evening parties are numerous, to present yourself at two or three houses during a single evening.

When your name is announced, look for the lady of the house, and pay your respects to her before you even seem to see any other of your friends who may be in the room. At very large and fashionable receptions, the hostess is generally to be found near the door. Should you, however, find yourself separated by a dense crowd of guests, you are at liberty to recognize those who are near you, and those whom you encounter as you make your way slowly through the throng.

If you are at the house of a new acquaintance and find yourself among entire strangers, remember that by so meeting under one roof you are all in a certain sense made known to one another, and should, therefore, converse freely, as equals. To shrink away to a side-table and affect to be absorbed in some album or illustrated work; or, if you find one unlucky acquaintance in the room to fasten upon her like a drowning man clinging to a spar, are *gaucheries* which no shyness can excuse.

If you possess any musical accomplishments, do not wait to be pressed and entreated by your hostess, but comply immediately when she pays you the compliment of inviting you to play or sing. Remember, however, that only the lady of the house has the right to ask you. If others do so, you can put them off in some polite way, but must not comply till the hostess herself invites you.

Be scrupulous to observe silence when any of the company are playing or singing. Remember that they are doing this for the amusement of the rest; and that to talk at such a time is as ill-bred as if you were to turn your back upon a person who was talking to you and begin a conversation with some one else.

If you are yourself the performer, bear in mind that in music, as in speech, "brevity is the soul of wit." Two verses of a song, or four pages of a piece, are at all times enough to give pleasure. If your audience desire more they will ask for it; and it is infinitely more flattering to be encored than to receive the thanks of your hearers, not so much in gratitude for what you have given them, but in relief that you have left off. You should try to suit your music, like your conversation, to your company. A solo of Beethoven's would be as much out of place in some circles as a comic song at a Quakers' meeting. To those who only care for the light popularities of the season, give Verdi, Suppé, Sullivan, or Offenbach. To connoisseurs, if you perform well enough to venture, give such music as will be likely to meet the exigencies of a fine taste. Above all, attempt nothing that you cannot execute with ease and precision.

If the party be of a small and social kind and those games called by the French *les jeux innocents* are proposed, do not object to join in them when invited. It may be that they demand some slight exercise of wit and readiness, and that you do not feel yourself calculated to shine in them; but it is better to seem dull than disagreeable, and those who are obliging can always find some clever neighbor to assist them in the moment of need.

Impromptu charades are frequently organized at friendly parties. Unless you have really some talent for acting and some readiness of speech, you should remember that you only put others out and expose your own inability by taking part in these entertainments. Of course, if your help is really needed, and you would disoblige by refusing, you must do your best, and by doing it as quietly and coolly as possible, avoid being awkward or ridiculous.

Even though you may take no pleasure in cards, some knowledge of the etiquette and rules belonging to the games most in vogue is necessary to you in society. If a fourth hand is wanted at euchre, or if the rest of the company sit down to a round game, you would be deemed guilty of an impoliteness if you refused to join.

The games most commonly played in society are euchre, draw-poker, and whist.

THE DINNER-PARTY.

To be acquainted with every detail of the etiquette pertaining to this subject is of the highest importance to every lady. Ease, *savoir-faire*, and good-breeding are nowhere more indispensable than at the dinner-table, and the absence of them is nowhere more apparent. How to eat soup and what to do with a cherry-stone are weighty considerations when taken as the index of social status; and it is not too much to say, that a young woman who elected to take claret with her fish, or ate peas with her knife, would justly risk the punishment of being banished from good society.

An invitation to dinner should be replied to immediately, and unequivocally accepted or declined. Once accepted, nothing but an event of the last importance should cause you to fail in your engagement.

To be exactly punctual is the strictest politeness on these occasions. If you are too early, you are in the way; if too late you spoil the dinner, annoy the hostess, and are hated by the rest of the guests. Some authorities are even of opinion that in the question of a dinner-party "never" is better than "late"; and one author has gone so far as to say, "if you do not reach the house till dinner is served, you had better retire, and send an apology, and not interrupt the harmony of the courses by awkward excuses and cold acceptance."

When the party is assembled, the mistress or master of the house will point out to each gentleman the lady whom he is to conduct to the table.

The lady who is the greatest stranger should be taken down by the master of the house, and the gentleman who is the greatest stranger should conduct the hostess. Married ladies take precedence of single ladies, elder ladies of younger ones, and so forth.

When dinner is announced, the host offers his arm to the lady of most distinction, invites the rest to follow by a few words or a bow, and leads the way. The lady of the house should then follow with the gentleman who is most entitled to that honor, and the visitors follow in the order that has been previously arranged. The lady of the house frequently remains, however, till the last, that she may see her guests go in their prescribed order; but the plan is not a convenient one. It is much better that the hostesss should be in her place as the guests enter the dining-room, in order that she may indicate their seats to them as they enter, and not find them all crowded together in uncertainty when she arrives.

The plan of cards, with the names of the guests on them, opposite their chairs, is a very useful one.

The lady of the house takes the head of the table. The gentleman who led her down to dinner occupies the seat on her right hand, and the gentleman next in order of precedence, that on her left. The master of the house takes the foot of the table. The lady whom he escorted sits on his right hand, and the lady next in order of precedence on his left.

As soon as you are seated at table, remove your gloves, place your table napkin across your knees, and remove the roll which you will probably find within it to the left side of your plate.

The soup should be placed on the table first. All well-ordered dinners begin with soup, whether in summer or winter. The lady of the house should help it, and send it round without asking each individual in turn. It is as much an understood thing as the bread beside each plate, and those who do not choose it are always at liberty to leave it untasted.

In eating soup, remember always to take it from the side of the spoon, and to make no sound in doing so.

If the servants do not go round with wine, the gentlemen should help the ladies and themselves to sherry or sauterne immediately after the soup.

You should never ask for a second supply of either soup or fish; it delays the next course, and keeps the table waiting.

Never offer to "assist" your neighbors to this or that dish. The word is inexpressibly vulgar—all the more vulgar for its affectation of elegance. "Shall I send you some mutton?" or "may I help you to canvas back?" is better chosen and better bred.

As a general rule, it is better not to ask your guests if they will partake of the dishes; but to send the plates round, and let them accept or decline them as they please. At very large dinners it is sometimes customary to distribute little lists of the order of the dishes at intervals along the table. It must be confessed that this gives somewhat the air of a dinner at an hotel; but it has the advantage of enabling the visitors to select their fare, and, as "forewarned is forearmed," to keep a corner, as the children say, for their favorite dishes.

As soon as you are helped, begin to eat; or, if the viands are too hot for your palate, take up your knife and fork and appear to begin. To wait for others is now not only old-fashioned, but ill-bred.

Never offer to pass on the plate to which you have been helped.

In helping soup, fish, or any other dish, remember that to overfill a plate is as bad as to supply it too scantily.

Silver fish knives will now always be met with at the best tables; but where there are none, a piece of crust should be taken in the left hand, and the fork in the right. There is no exception to this rule in eating fish.

We presume it is scarcely necessary to remind our fair reader that she is never, under any circumstances, to convey her knife to her mouth. Peas are eaten with the fork; tarts, curry, and puddings of all kinds with the spoon.

Always help fish with a fish-slice, and tart and puddings with a spoon, or, if necessary, a spoon and fork.

Asparagus must be helped with the asparagus-tongs.

In eating asparagus, it is well to observe what others do, and act accordingly. Some very well-bred people eat it with the fingers; others cut off the heads, and convey them to the mouth upon the fork. If would be difficult to say which is the more correct.

In eating stone fruit, such as cherries, damsons, etc., the same rule had better be observed. Some put the stones out from the mouth into a spoon, and so convey them to the plate. Others cover the lips with the hand, drop them unseen into the palm, and so deposit them on the side of the plate. In our own opinion, the latter is the better way, as it effectually conceals the return of the stones, which is certainly the point of highest importance. Of one thing we may be sure, and that is, that they must never be dropped from the mouth to the plate.

In helping sauce, always pour it on the side of the plate.

If the servants do not go round with the wine (which is by far the best custom), the gentlemen at a dinner-table should take upon themselves the office of helping those ladies who sit near them.

Unless you are a total abstainer, it is extremely uncivil to decline taking wine if you are invited to do so.

It is particularly ill-bred to empty your glass on these occasions.

Certain wines are taken with certain dishes, by old-established custom—as sherry or sauterne, with soup and fish; hock and claret with roast meat; punch with turtle; champagne with sweet-bread or cutlets; port with venison; port or burgundy, with game; sparkling wines between the roast and the confectionery; madeira with sweets; port with cheese; and for dessert, port, tokay, madeira, sherry, and claret. Red wines should never be iced, even in summer. Claret and burgundy should always be slightly warmed; claret-cup and champagne should, of course, be iced.

Instead of cooling their wines in the ice-pail, some hosts introduce clear ice upon the table, broken up in small lumps, to be put inside the glasses. This cannot be too strictly reprehended. Melting ice can but weaken the quality and flavor of the wine. Those who desire to drink *wine and water* can ask for iced water if they choose; but it savors too much of economy on the part of a host to insinuate the ice inside the glasses of his guests when the wine could be more effectually iced outside the bottle.

A silver knife and fork should be placed to each guest at dessert.

It is wise never to partake of any dish without knowing of what ingredients it is composed. You can always ask the servant who hands it to you, and you thereby avoid all danger of having to commit the impoliteness of leaving it, and showing that you do not approve of it.

Never speak while you have anything in your mouth.

Be careful never to taste soups or puddings till you are sure they are sufficiently cool ; as, by disregarding this caution, you may be compelled to swallow what is dangerously hot, or be driven to the unpardonable alternative of returning it to your plate.

When eating or drinking, avoid every kind of audible testimony to the fact.

Finger-glasses, containing water slightly warmed and perfumed, are placed to each person at dessert. In these you may dip the tips of your fingers, wiping them afterwards on your table-napkin. If the finger-glass and doyley are placed on your dessert-plate, you should immediately remove the doyley to the left of your plate, and place the finger-glass upon it. By these means you leave the right for the wine-glasses.

Be careful to know the shapes of the various kinds of wine-glasses commonly in use, in order that you may never put forward one for another. High and narrow, and very broad and shallow glasses, are used for champagne ; large goblet-shaped glasses for burgundy and claret ; ordinary wine-glasses for sherry and madeira ; green glasses for hock ; and somewhat large, bell-shaped glasses for port.

Port, sherry, and madeira are decanted. Hocks and champagnes appear in their native bottles. Claret and burgundy are handed round in a claret-jug.

The servants leave the room when the dessert is on the table.

Coffee and liqueurs should be handed round when the dessert has been about a quarter of an hour on the table. After this the ladies generally retire.

The lady of the house should never send away her plate, or appear to have done eating, till all her guests have finished.

If you should unfortunately overturn or break anything, do not apologize for it. You can show your regret in your face, but it is not well-bred to put it into words.

To abstain from taking the last piece on the dish, or the last glass of wine in the decanter, only because it is the last, is highly ill-bred. It implies a fear on your part that the vacancy cannot be supplied, and almost conveys an affront to your host.

To those ladies who have houses and servants at command, we have one or two remarks to offer. Every housekeeper should be acquainted with the routine of a dinner and the etiquette of a dinner-table. No lady should be utterly dependent on the taste and judgment of her cook. Though she need not know how to dress a dish, she should be able to judge of it when served. The mistress of the house, in short, should be to a cook what a publisher is to his authors—that is to say, competent to form a judgment upon their works, though himself incapable of writing even a magazine article.

If you wish to have a good dinner, and do not know in what manner to set about it, you will do wisely to order it from some first-rate *restaurateur*. By these means you insure the best cookery and a faultless *carte*.

Bear in mind that it is your duty to entertain your friends in the best manner that your means permit. This is the least you can do to recompense them for the expenditure of time and money which they incur in accepting your invitation.

"To invite a friend to dinner," says Brillat Savarin, "is to become responsible for his happiness so long as he is under your roof."

A dinner, to be excellent, need not consist of a great variety of dishes ; but everything should be of the best, and the cookery should be perfect. That which should be cool should be cool as ice ; that which should be hot should be smoking ; the attendance should be rapid and noiseless ; the guests well assorted ; the wines of the best quality ; the host attentive and courteous ; the room well lighted, and the time punctual.

Every dinner should begin with soup, be followed by fish, and include some kind of game. "The soup is to the dinner," we are told by Grisnod de la Regnière, "what the portico is to a building, or the overture to an opera."

To this aphorism we may be permitted to add that a *chasse* of cognac or curaçoa at the close of a dinner is like the epilogue at the end of a comedy.

Never reprove or give directions to your servants before guests. If a dish is not placed precisely where you would have wished it to stand, or the order of a course is reversed, let the error pass unobserved by yourself, and you may depend that it will be unnoticed by others.

The duties of hostess at a dinner-party are not onerous ; but they demand tact and good breeding, grace of bearing, and self-possession of no ordinary degree. She does not often carve. She has no active duties to perform ; but she must neglect nothing, forget nothing, put all her guests at their ease, encourage the timid, draw out the silent, and pay every possible attention to the requirements of each and all around her. No accident must ruffle her temper. No disappointment must embarrass her. She must see her old china broken without a sigh, and her best glass shattered with a smile.

STAYING AT A FRIEND'S HOUSE—BREAKFAST, LUNCHEON, ETC.

A visitor is bound by the laws of social intercourse to conform in all respects to the habits of the house. In order to do this effectually, she should inquire, or cause her personal servant to inquire, what those habits are. To keep your friend's breakfast on the table till a late hour ; to delay the dinner by want of punctuality ; to accept other invitations, and treat his house as if it were merely an hotel to be slept in ; or to keep the family up till unwonted hours, are alike evidences of a want of good feeling and good-breeding.

At breakfast and lunch absolute punctuality is not imperative ; but a visitor should avoid being always the last to appear at table.

No order of precedence is observed at either breakfast or luncheon. Persons take their seats as they come in, and, having exchanged their morning salutations, begin to eat without waiting for the rest of the party.

If letters are delivered to you at breakfast or luncheon, you may read them by asking permission from the lady who presides at the urn.

Always hold yourself at the disposal of those in whose house you are visiting. If they propose to ride, drive, walk, or otherwise occupy the day, you may take it for granted that these plans are made with reference to your enjoyment. You should, therefore, receive them with cheerfulness, enter into them with alacrity, and do your best to seem pleased, and be pleased, by the efforts which your friends make to entertain you.

You should never take a book from the library to your own room without requesting permission to borrow it. When it is lent, you should take every care that it sustains no injury while in your possession, and should cover it, if necessary.

A guest should endeavor to amuse herself as much as possible, and not be continually dependent on her hosts for entertainment. She should remember that, however welcome she may be, she is not always wanted.

A visitor should avoid giving unnecessary trouble to the servants of the house.

The signal for retiring to rest is generally given by the appearance of the servant with wine, water, and biscuits, where a late dinner hour is observed and suppers are not the custom. This is the last refreshment of the evening, and the visitor will do well to rise and wish good night shortly after it has been partaken of by the family.

GENERAL HINTS.

Do not frequently repeat the name of the person with whom you are conversing. It implies either the extreme of *hauteur* or familiarity.

Never speak of absent persons by only their Christian or surnames; but always as Mr. ——, or Mrs. ——. Above all, never name anybody by the first letter of his name. Married people are sometimes guilty of this flagrant offense against taste.

Look at those who address you.

Never boast of your birth, your money, your grand friends, or anything that is yours. If you have traveled, do not introduce that information into your conversation at every opportunity. Any one can travel with money and leisure. The real distinction is to come home with enlarged views, improved tastes, and a mind free from prejudice.

If you present a book to a friend, do not write his or her name in it, unless requested. You have no right to presume that it will be rendered any the more valuable for that addition; and you ought not to conclude beforehand that your gift will be accepted.

Never undervalue the gift which you are yourself offering: you have no business to offer it if it is valueless. Neither say that you do not want it yourself, or that you should throw it away if it were not accepted, etc., etc. Such apologies would be insults if true, and mean nothing if false.

No compliment that bears insincerity on the face of it is a compliment at all.

Presents made by a married lady to a gentleman can only be offered in the joint names of her husband and herself.

Married ladies may occasionally accept presents from gentlemen who visit frequently at their houses, and who desire to show their sense of the hospitality which they receive there.

Acknowledge the receipt of a present without delay.

Give a foreigner his name in full, as Monsieur de Vigny—never as *Monsieur* only. In speaking of him, give him his title, if he has one. Foreign noblemen are addressed *viva voce* as Monsieur. In speaking of a foreign nobleman before his face, say Monsieur le Comte, or Monsieur le Marquis. In his absence, say Monsieur le Comte de Vigny.

Converse with a foreigner in his own language. If not competent to do so, apologize, and beg permission to speak English.

To get in and out of a carriage gracefully is a simple but important accomplishment. If there is but one step, and you are going to take the seat facing the horses, put your left foot on the step, and enter the carriage with your right, in such a manner as to drop at once into your seat. If you are about to sit with your back to the horses, reverse the process. As you step into the carriage, be careful to keep your back towards the seat you are about to occupy, so as to avoid the awkwardness of turning when you are once in.

ETIQUETTE FOR GENTLEMEN.

INTRODUCTIONS.

To introduce persons who are mutually unknown is to undertake a serious responsibility, and to certify to each the respectability of the other. Never undertake this responsibility without in the first place asking yourself whether the persons are likely to be agreeable to each other; nor, in the second place, without ascertaining whether it will be acceptable to both parties to become acquainted.

Always introduce the gentleman to the lady—never the lady to the gentleman. The chivalry of etiquette assumes that the lady is invariably the superior in right of her sex, and that the gentleman is honored by the introduction.

Never present a gentleman to a lady without first asking her permission to do so.

When you are introduced to a lady, never offer your hand. When introduced, persons limit their recognition of each other to a bow.

Persons who have met at the house of a mutual friend without being introduced, should not bow if they afterwards meet elsewhere; a bow implies acquaintance, and persons who have not been introduced are not acquainted.

If you are walking with one friend, and presently meet with, or are joined by, a second, do not commit the too frequent error of introducing them to each other. You have even less right to do so than if they encountered each other at your house during a morning call.

There are some exceptions to the etiquette of introductions. At a ball or evening party, where there is dancing, the mistress of the house may introduce any gentleman to any lady without first asking the lady's permission. But she should first ascertain whether the lady is willing to dance; and this out of consideration for the gentleman, who may otherwise be refused. No man likes to be refused the hand of a lady, though it be only for a quadrille.

A brother may present his sister, or a father his son, without any kind of preliminary: but only when there is no inferiority on the part of his own family to that of the acquaintance.

Friends may introduce friends at the house of a mutual acquaintance, but, as a rule, it is better to be introduced by the mistress of the house. Such an introduction carries more authority with it.

Introductions at evening parties are now almost wholly dispensed with. Persons who meet at a friend's house are ostensibly upon an equality, and pay a bad compliment to the host by appearing suspicious and formal. Some old-fashioned country hosts yet persevere in introducing each newcomer to all the assembled guests. It is a custom that cannot be too soon abolished, and one that places the last unfortunate visitor in a singularly awkward position. All that he can do is to make a semicircular bow, like a concert singer before an audience, and bear the general gaze with as much composure as possible.

If, when you enter a drawing-room, your name has been wrongly announced, or has passed unheard in the buzz of conversation, make your way at once to the mistress of the house, if you are a stranger, and introduce yourself by name. This should be done with the greatest simplicity, and your professional or titular rank made as little of as possible.

An introduction given at a ball for the mere purpose of conducting a lady through a dance does not give the gentleman any right to bow to her on a future occasion. If he commits this error, he must remember that she is not bound to see or return his salutation.

LETTERS OF INTRODUCTION.

Do not lightly give or promise letters of introduction. Always remember that when you give a letter of introduction you lay yourself under an obligation to the friend to whom it is addressed.

No one delivers a letter of introduction in person. It places you in the most undignified position imaginable, and compels you to wait while it is being read, like a footman who has been told to wait for an answer.

If, on the other hand, a stranger sends you a letter of introduction and his card, you are bound by the laws of politeness and hospitality, not only to call upon him the next day, but to follow up that attention with others. If you are in a position to do so, the most correct proceeding is to invite him to dine with you. Should this not be within your power, you have probably the *entrée* to some private collections, club-houses, theaters, or reading-rooms, and could devote a few hours to showing him these places.

A letter of introduction should be given unsealed, not alone because your friend may wish to know what you have said of him, but also as a guarantee of your own good faith. As you should never give such a letter unless you can speak highly of the bearer, this rule of etiquette is easy to observe. By requesting your friend to fasten the envelope before forwarding the letter to its destination you tacitly give him permission to inspect its contents.

Let your note paper be of the best quality and proper size.

VISITING.—MORNING CALLS.—CARDS.

A morning visit should be paid between the hours of 2 and 4 P.M. in winter, and 2 and 5 in summer.

Visits of ceremony should be short. If even the conversation should have become animated, beware of letting your call exceed half an hour's length. It is always better to let your friends regret rather than desire your withdrawal.

On returning visits of ceremony you may, without impoliteness, leave your card at the door without going in. Do not fail, however, to inquire if the family be well.

Should there be daughters or sisters residing with the lady upon whom you call, you may turn down a corner of your card, to signify that the visit is paid to all. It is in better taste, however, to leave cards for each.

Unless when returning thanks for "kind inquiries," or announcing your arrival in, or departure from, town, it is not considered respectful to send cards round by a servant.

Leave-taking cards have P.P.C. (*pour prendre congé*) written in the corner. Some use P.D.A. (*pour dire adieu*).

The visiting cards of gentlemen are half the size of those used by ladies.

Visits of condolence are paid within the week after the event which occasions them. Personal visits of this kind are made by relations and very intimate friends only. Acquaintances should leave cards with narrow mourning borders.

On the first occasion when you are received by the family after the death of one of its members, it is etiquette to wear slight mourning.

When a gentleman makes a morning call, he should never leave his hat or riding-whip in the hall, but should take both into the room. To do otherwise would be to make himself too much at home. The hat, however, must never be laid on a table, piano, or any article of furniture, it should be held gracefully in the hand. If you are compelled to lay it aside put it on the floor.

Umbrellas should invariably be left in the hall.

Never take favorite dogs into a drawing-room when you make a morning call. Their feet may be dusty, or they may bark at the sight of strangers, or, being of too friendly a disposition, may take the liberty of lying on a lady's gown, or jumping on the sofas and easy chairs. Where your friend has a favorite cat already established before the fire, a battle may ensue, and one or both of the pets be seriously hurt. Besides, many persons have a constitutional antipathy to dogs, and others never allow their own to be seen in the sitting-rooms. For all or any of these reasons a visitor has no right to inflict upon his friend the society of his dog as well as of himself.

If, when you call upon a lady, you meet a lady visitor in her drawing-room, you should rise when that lady takes her leave.

If other visitors are announced, and you have already remained as long as courtesy requires, wait till they are seated, and then rise from your chair, take leave of your hostess, and bow politely to the newly arrived guests. You will, perhaps, be urged to remain, but, having once risen, it is always best to go. There is always a certain air of *gaucherie* in resuming your seat and repeating the ceremony of leave taking.

If you have occasion to look at your watch during a call, ask permission to do so, and apologize for it on the plea of other appointments.

CONVERSATION.

Let your conversation be adapted as skillfully as may be to your company. Some men make a point of talking commonplaces to all ladies alike, as if a woman could only be a trifler. Others, on the contrary, seem to forget in what respects the education of a lady differs from that of a gentleman, and commit the opposite error of conversing on topics with which ladies are seldom acquainted. A woman of sense has as much right to be annoyed by the one, as a lady of ordinary education by the other. You cannot pay a finer compliment to a woman of refinement and *esprit* than by leading the conversation into such a channel as may mark your appreciation of her superior attainments.

In talking with ladies of ordinary education, avoid political, scientific, or commercial topics, and choose only such subjects as are likely to be of interest to them.

Remember that people take more interest in their own affairs than in anything else which you can name. If you wish your conversation to be thoroughly agreeable, lead a mother to talk of her children, a young lady of her last ball, an author of his forthcoming book, or an artist of his exhibition picture. Having furnished the topic, you need only listen; and you are sure to be thought not only agreeable, but thoroughly sensible and well-informed.

Be careful, however, on the other hand, not always to make a point of talking to persons upon general matters relating to their professions. To show an interest in their immediate concerns is flattering; but to converse with them too much about their own arts looks as if you thought them ignorant of other topics.

Do not use a classical quotation in the presence of ladies without apologizing for, or translating it. Even this should only be done when no other phrase would so aptly express your meaning. Whether in the presence of ladies or gentlemen, much display of learning is pedantic and out of place.

There is a certain distinct but subdued tone of voice which is peculiar to only well-bred persons. A loud voice is both disagreeable and vulgar. It is better to err by the use of too low rather than too loud a tone.

Remember that all "slang" is vulgar.

Do not pun. Puns unless they rise to the rank of witticisms, are to be scrupulously avoided.

Long arguments in general company, however entertaining to the disputants, are tiresome to the last degree to all others. You should always endeavor to prevent the conversation from dwelling too long upon one topic.

Religion is a topic which should never be introduced in society. It is the one subject on which persons are most likely to differ, and least able to preserve temper.

Never interrupt a person who is speaking.

To listen well, is almost as great an art as to talk well. It is not enough *only* to listen. You must endeavor to seem interested in the conversation of others.

It is considered extremely ill-bred when two persons whisper in society, or converse in a language with which all present are not familiar. If you have private matters to discuss, you should appoint a proper time and place to do so, without paying others the ill compliment of excluding them from your conversation.

If a foreigner be one of the guests at a small-party, and does not understand English sufficiently to follow what is said, good-breeding demands that the conversation shall be carried on in his own language. If at a dinner-party, the same rule applies to those at his end of the table.

If upon the entrance of a visitor you carry on the thread of a previous conversation, you should briefly recapitulate to him what has been said before he arrived.

Always look, but never stare, at those with whom you converse.

In order to meet the general needs of conversation in society, it is necessary that a man should be well acquainted with the current news and historical events of at least the last few years.

Never talk upon subjects of which you know nothing, unless it be for the purpose of acquiring information. Many young men imagine that because they frequent exhibitions and operas they are qualified judges of art. No mistake is more egregious or universal.

Those who introduce anecdotes into their conversation are warned that these should invariably be "short, witty, eloquent, new, and not far-fetched."

Scandal is the least excusable of all conversational vulgarities.

In conversing with a man of rank, do not too frequently give him his title.

THE PROMENADE.

A well-bred man must entertain no respect for the brim of his hat. "A bow," says La Fontaine, "is a note drawn at sight." You are bound to acknowledge it immediately, and to the full amount. True politeness demands that the hat should be quite lifted from the head.

On meeting friends with whom you are likely to shake hands, remove your hat with the left hand in order to leave the right hand free.

If you meet a lady in the street whom you are sufficiently intimate to address, do not stop her, but turn round and walk beside her in whichever direction she is going. When you have said all that you wish to say, you can take your leave.

If you meet a lady with whom you are not particularly well acquainted, wait for her recognition before you venture to bow to her.

In bowing to a lady whom you are not going to address, lift your hat with that hand which is farthest from her. For instance, if you pass her on the right side, use your left hand; if on the left, use your right.

If you are on horseback and wish to converse with a lady who is on foot, you must dismount and lead your horse, so as not to give her the fatigue of looking up to your level. Neither should you subject her to the impropriety of carrying on a conversation in a tone necessarily louder than is sanctioned in public by the laws of good breeding.

When you meet friends or acquaintances in the streets, at the exhibitions, or any public places, take care not to pronounce their names so loudly as to attract the attention of the passers-by. Never call across the street; and never carry on a dialogue in a public vehicle, unless your interlocutor occupies the seat beside your own.

In walking with a lady, take charge of any small parcel, parasol, or book with which she may be encumbered.

DRESS.

A gentleman should always be so well dressed that his dress shall never be observed at all. Does this sound like an enigma? It is not meant for one. It only implies that perfect simplicity is perfect elegance, and that the true test of taste in the toilet of a gentleman is its entire harmony, unobtrusiveness, and becomingness. If any friend should say to you, "What a handsome waistcoat you have on!" you may depend that a less handsome waistcoat would be in better taste. If you hear it said that Mr. So-and-So wears superb jewelry, you may conclude beforehand that he wears too much. Display, in short, is ever to be avoided, especially in matters of dress. The toilet is the domain of the fair sex. Let a wise man leave its graces and luxuries to his wife, daughters, or sisters, and seek to be himself appreciated for something of higher worth than the stud in his shirt or the trinkets on his chain.

To be too much in the fashion is as vulgar as to be too far behind it. No really well-bred man follows every new cut that he sees in his tailor's fashion-book.

In the morning wear frock coats, double-breasted waistcoats, and trousers of light or dark colors, according to the season.

In the evening, though only in the bosom of your own family, wear only black, and be as scrupulous to put on a dress coat as if you expected visitors. If you have sons, bring them up to do the same. It is the observance of these minor trifles in domestic etiquette which marks the true gentleman.

For evening parties, dinner parties, and balls, wear a black dress coat, black trousers, black silk or cloth waistcoat, white cravat, white or gray kid gloves, and thin patent leather boots.

A black cravat may be worn in full dress, but is not so elegant as a white one.

Let your jewelry be of the best, but the least gaudy description, and wear it very sparingly. A single stud, a gold watch and guard, and one handsome ring, are as many ornaments as a gentleman can wear with propriety.

It is well to remember in the choice of jewelry that mere costliness is not always the test of value; and that an exquisite work of art, such as a fine cameo, or a natural rarity, such as a black pearl, is a more *distingué* possession than a large brilliant, which any rich and tasteless vulgarian can buy as easily as yourself. For a ring, the gentleman of fine taste would prefer a precious antiqe *intaglio* to the handsomest diamond or ruby that could be bought at Tiffany's.

Of all precious stones, the opal is one of the most lovely and the least common-place. No vulgar man purchases an opal. He invariably prefers the more showy diamond, ruby, sapphire, or emerald.

Unless you are a snuff-taker, never carry any but a white pocket-handkerchief.

If in the morning you wear a long cravat fastened by a pin, be careful to avoid what may be called *alliteration* of color. We have seen a turquois pin worn in a violet-colored cravat, and the effect was frightful. Choose, if possible, complementary colors, and their secondaries. For instance, if the stone in your pin be a turquois, wear it with brown, or crimson mixed with black, or black and orange. If a ruby, contrast it with shades of green. The same rule holds good with regard to the mixture and contrast of colors in your waistcoat and cravat. Thus, a buff waistcoat and a blue tie, or brown and blue, or brown and green, or brown and magenta, green and magenta, green and mauve, are all good arrangements of color.

Colored shirts may be worn in the morning; but they should be small in pattern and quiet in color.

In these days of public baths and universal progress, we trust that it is unnecessary to do more than hint at the necessity of the most fastidious personal cleanliness. The hair, the teeth, the nails, should be faultlessly kept; and a soiled shirt, a dingy pocket-handkerchief, or a light waistcoat that has been worn once too often, are things to be scrupulously avoided by any man who is ambitious of preserving the exterior of a gentleman.

RIDING AND DRIVING.

riding, as in walking, give the lady the wall.

If you assist a lady to mount, hold your hand at a convenient distance from the ground that she may place her foot in it. As she springs, you aid her by the impetus of your hand. In doing this, it is always better to agree upon a signal, that her spring and your assistance may come at the same moment.

For this purpose there is no better form than the old dueling one of "one, two, *three*."

When the lady is in the saddle, it is your place to find the stirrup for her, and guide her left foot to it. When this is done, she rises in her seat and you assist her to draw her habit straight.

Even when a groom is present, it is more polite for the gentleman himself to perform this office for his fair companion; as it would be more polite for him to hand her a chair than to have it handed by a servant.

If the lady be light, you must take care not to give her too much impetus in mounting. We have known a lady nearly thrown over her horse by a misplaced zeal of this kind.

If a gate has to be opened, we need hardly observe that it is your place to hold it open till the lady has passed through.

In driving, a gentleman places himself with his back to the horses, and leaves the best seat for the ladies.

When the carriage stops, the gentleman should alight first, in order to assist the lady.

To get in and out of a carriage gracefully is a simple but important accomplishment. If there is but one step, and you are going to take your seat facing the horses, put your left foot on the step, and enter the carriage with your right in such a manner as to drop at once into your seat. If you are about to sit with your back to the horses, reverse the process. As you step into the carriage, be careful to keep your back towards the seat you are about to occupy, so as to avoid the awkwardness of turning when you are once in.

A gentleman cannot be too careful to avoid stepping on ladies' dresses when he gets in or out of a carriage. He should also beware of shutting them in with the door.

MORNING AND EVENING PARTIES.

Elegant morning dress, general good manners, and some acquaintance with the topics of the day and the games above named, are all the qualifications especially necessary to a gentleman at a morning party.

An evening party begins about nine o'clock P.M., and ends about midnight, or somewhat later. Good-breeding neither demands that you should present yourself at the commencement, nor remain till the close of the evening. You come and go as may be most convenient to you, and by these means are at liberty, during the height of the season when evening parties are numerous, to present yourself at two or three houses during a single evening.

At very large and fashionable receptions, the hostess is generally to be found near the door. Should you, however, find yourself separated by a dense crowd of guests, you are at liberty to recognize those who are near you, and those whom you encounter as you make your way slowly through the throng.

If you are at the house of a new acquaintance and find yourself among entire strangers, remember that by so meeting under one roof you are all in a certain sense made known to one another, and should therefore converse freely, as equals. To shrink away to a side-table and affect to be absorbed in some album or illustrated work; or, if you find one unlucky acquaintance in the room, to fasten upon him like a drowning man clinging to a spar, are *gaucheries* which no shyness can excuse. An easy and unembarrassed manner, and the self-possession requisite to open a conversation with those who happen to be near you, are the indispensable credentials of a well-bred man.

At an evening party, do not remain too long in one spot

To be afraid to move from one drawing-room to another is the sure sign of a neophyte in society.

If you have occasion to use your handkerchief, do so as noiselessly as possible. To blow your nose as if it were a trombone, or to turn your head aside when using your handkerchief, are vulgarities scrupulously to be avoided.

Never stand upon the hearth with your back to the fire or stove, either in a friend's house or your own.

Never offer any one the chair from which you have just risen, unless there be no other disengaged.

If, when supper is announced, no lady has been specially placed under your care by the hostess, offer your arm to whichever lady you may have last conversed with.

If you possess any musical accomplishments, do not wait to be pressed and entreated by your hostess, but comply immediately when she pays you the compliment of inviting you to play or sing. Remember, however, that only the lady of the house has the right to ask you. If others do so, you can put them off in some polite way; but must not comply till the hostess herself invites you.

If you sing comic songs, be careful that they are of the most unexceptionable kind, and likely to offend neither the tastes nor prejudices of the society in which you find yourself.

If the party be of a small and social kind, and those games called by the French *les jeux innocents* are proposed, do not object to join in them when invited. It may be that they demand some slight exercise of wit and readiness, and that you do not feel yourself calculated to shine in them; but it is better to seem dull than disagreeable, and those who are obliging can always find some clever neighbor to assist them in the moment of need. The game of "consequences" is one which unfortunately gives too much scope to liberty of expression. If you join in this game, we cannot too earnestly enjoin you never to write down one word which the most pure-minded woman present might not read aloud without a blush. Jests of an equivocal character are not only vulgar, but contemptible.

Impromptu charades are frequently organized at friendly parties. Unless you have really some talent for acting and some readiness of speech, you should remember that you only put others out and expose your own inability by taking part in these entertainments. Of course, if your help is really needed and you would disoblige by refusing, you must do your best, and by doing it as quietly and coolly as possible, avoid being awkward or ridiculous.

Should an impromptu polka or quadrille be got up after supper at a party where no dancing was intended, be sure not to omit putting on gloves before you stand up. It is well always to have a pair of white gloves in your pocket in case of need; but even black are better under these circumstances than none.

Even though you may take no pleasure in cards, some knowledge of the etiquette and rules belonging to the games most in vogue is necessary to you in society.

Never let even politeness induce you to play for high stakes. Etiquette is the minor morality of life; but it never should be allowed to outweigh the higher code of right and wrong.

Be scrupulous to observe silence when any of the company are playing or singing. Remember that they are doing this for the amusement of the rest; and that to talk at such a time is as ill-bred as if you were to turn your back upon a person who was talking to you, and begin a conversation with some one else.

If you are yourself the performer, bear in mind that in music, as in speech, "brevity is the soul of wit." Two verses of a song, or four pages of a piece, are at all times enough to give pleasure. If your audience desire more they will ask for it; and it is infinitely more flattering to be encored than to receive the thanks of you hearers, not so much in gratitude for what you have given them, but in relief that you have left off. You should try to suit your music, like your conversation, to your company. A solo of Beethoven's would be as much out of place in some circles as a comic song at a Quakers' meeting. To those who only care for the light popularities of the season, give Verdi. To connoisseurs, if you perform well enough to venture, give such music as will be likely to meet the exigencies of a fine taste. Above all, attempt nothing that you cannot execute with ease and precision.

In retiring from a crowded party it is unnecessary that you should seek out the hostess for the purpose of bidding her a formal good-night. By doing this you would, perhaps, remind others that it was getting late, and cause the party to break up. If you meet the lady of the house on your way to the drawing-room door, take your leave of her as unobtrusively as possible, and slip away without attracting the attention of her other guests.

THE DINNER TABLE.

To be acquainted with every detail of the etiquette pertaining to this subject is of the highest importance to every gentleman. Ease, *savoir faire*, and good-breeding are nowhere more indispensable than at the dinner-table, and the absence of them is nowhere more apparent.

An invitation to dine should be replied to immediately, and unequivocally accepted or declined. Once accepted, nothing but an event of the last importance should cause you to fail in your engagement.

To be exactly punctual is the strictest politeness on these occasions. If you are too early, you are in the way; if too late, you spoil the dinner, annoy the hostess, and are hated by the rest of the guests. Some authorities are even of opinion that in the question of a dinner-party "never" is better than "late"; and one author has gone so far as to say, "if you do not reach the house till dinner is served, you had better retire to a restaurateur's, and thence send an apology, and not interrupt the harmony of the courses by awkward excuses and cold acceptance."

When the party is assembled, the mistress or master of the house will point out to each gentleman the lady whom he is to conduct to table. If she be a stranger, you had better seek an introduction; if a previous acquaintance, take care to be near her when the dinner is announced; offer your arm, and go down according to precedence. This order of precedence must be arranged by the host or hostess.

When dinner is announced, the host offers his arm to the lady of most distinction, invites the rest to follow by a few words or a bow, and leads the way. The lady of the house should then follow with the gentleman who is most entitled to that honor, and the visitors follow in the order that the master of the house has previously arranged. The lady of the house frequently remains, however, till the last, that she may see her guests go down in their prescribed order; but the plan is not a convenient one. It is much better that the hostess should be in her place as the guests enter the dining-room, in order that she may indicate their seats to them as they come in, and not find them all crowded together in uncertainty when she arrives. If cards with names are on the table seek that of the lady whom you have taken to dinner.

The number of guests at a dinner-party should always be determined by the size of the table. When the party is too small, conversation flags, and a general air of desolation pervades the table. When they are too many, every one is inconvenienced. A space of two feet should be allowed to each person. It is well to arrange a party in such wise that the number of ladies and gentlemen be equal.

The lady of the house takes the head of the table. The gentleman who led her down to dinner occupies the seat on her right hand, and the gentleman next in order of precedence that on her left. The master of the house takes the foot of the table. The lady whom he escorted sits on his right hand, and the lady next in order of precedence on his left.

The gentlemen who support the lady of the house should offer to relieve her of the duties of hostess. Many ladies are well pleased thus to delegate the difficulties of carving, and all gentlemen who accept invitations to dinner should be prepared to render such assistance when called upon. To offer to carve a dish, and then perform the office unskillfully, is an unpardonable *gaucherie*. Every gentleman should carve, and carve well.

As soon as you are seated at table, remove your gloves, place your table napkin across your knees, and remove the roll which you find probably within it to the left side of your plate.

The soup should be placed on the table first.

In eating soup, remember always to take it from the side of the spoon, and to make no sound in doing so.

If the servants do not go round with wine the gentlemen should help the ladies and themselves to sherry or sauterne immediately after the soup.

You should never ask for a second supply of either soup or fish; it delays the next course and keeps the table waiting.

Never offer to "assist" your neighbors to this or that dish. The word is inexpressibly vulgar—all the more vulgar for its affectation of elegance. "Shall I send you some mutton?" or "may I help you to canvas back?" is better chosen and better bred.

If you are asked to take wine, it is polite to select the same as that which your interlocutor is drinking. If you invite a lady to take wine, you should ask her which she will prefer, and then take the same yourself. Should you, however, for any reason prefer some other vintage, you can take it by courteously requesting her permission.

As soon as you are helped, begin to eat; or, if the viands are too hot for your palate, take up your knife and fork and appear to begin. To wait for others is now not only old-fashioned, but ill-bred.

Never offer to pass on the plate to which you have been helped.

In helping soup, fish, or any other dish, remember that to overfill a plate is as bad as to supply it too scantily.

Silver fish-knives will now always be met with at the best tables; but where there are none, a piece of crust should be taken in the left hand, and the fork in the right. There is no exception to this rule in eating fish.

We presume it is scarcely necessary to remind the reader that he is never, under any circumstances, to convey his knife to his mouth. Peas are eaten with the fork; tarts, curry, and puddings of all kinds with the spoon.

Always help fish with a fish-slice, and tart and puddings with a spoon, or, if necessary, a spoon and fork.

Asparagus must be helped with the asparagus-tongs.

In eating asparagus, it is well to observe what others do, and act accordingly. Some very well-bred people eat it with the fingers; others cut off the heads, and convey them to the mouth upon the fork. It would be difficult to say which is the more correct.

In eating stone fruit, such as cherries, damsons, etc., the same rule had better be observed. Some put the stones out from the mouth into a spoon, and so convey them to the plate. Others cover the lips with the hand, drop them unseen into the palm, and so deposit them on the side of the plate. In our own opinion, the latter is the better way, as it effectually conceals the return of the stones, which is certainly the point of highest importance. Of one thing we may be sure, and that is, that they must never be dropped from the mouth to the plate.

In helping sauce, always pour it on the side of the plate.

If the servants do not go round with the wine (which is by far the best custom), the gentlemen at a dinner table should take upon themselves the office of helping those ladies who sit near them. Ladies take more wine in the present day than they did fifty years ago, and gentlemen should remember this, and offer it frequently. Ladies cannot very well ask for wine, but they can always decline it. At all events they do not like to be neglected, or to see gentlemen liberally helping themselves, without observing whether their fair neighbors' glasses are full or empty.

The habit of taking wine with each other has almost wholly gone out of fashion. A gentleman may ask the lady whom he conducted down to dinner, or he may ask the lady of the house to take wine with him. But even these last remnants of the old custom are fast falling into disuse.

Unless you are a total abstainer, it is extremely uncivil to decline taking wine if you are invited to do so. In accepting, you have only to pour a little fresh wine into your glass, look at the person who invited you, bow slightly, and take a sip from the glass.

It is particularly ill-bred to empty your glass on these occasions.

Certain wines are taken with certain dishes, by old-established custom—as sherry or sauterne, with soup and fish;

hock and claret, with roast meat; punch with turtle; champagne with sweet-bread and cutlets; port with venison; port or burgundy, with game; sparkling wines between the roast and the confectionery; madeira with sweets; port with cheese; and for dessert, port, tokay, madeira, sherry and claret. Red wines should never be iced, even in summer. Claret and burgundy should always be slightly warmed; claret-cup and champagne-cup should, of course, be iced.

Instead of cooling their wines in the ice pail, some hosts introduce clear ice upon the table, broken up in small lumps, to be put inside the glasses. This cannot be too strongly reprehended. Melting ice can but weaken the quality and flavor of the wine. Those who desire to drink *wine and water*, can ask for iced water if they choose, but it savors too much of economy on the part of the host to insinuate the ice inside the glasses of his guests when the wine could be more effectually iced outside the bottle.

A silver knife and fork should be placed to each guest at dessert.

If you are asked to prepare fruit for a lady, be careful to do so by means of the silver knife and fork only, and never to touch it with your fingers.

It is wise never to partake of any dish without knowing of what ingredients it is composed. You can always ask the servant who hands it to you, and you thereby avoid all danger of having to commit the impoliteness of leaving it, and showing that you do not approve of it.

Never speak while you have anything in your mouth.

Be careful never to taste soups or puddings till you are sure they are sufficiently cool; as, by disregarding this caution, you may be compelled to swallow what is dangerously hot. or be driven to the unpardonable alternative of returning it to your plate.

When eating or drinking, avoid every kind of audible testimony to the fact.

Finger-glasses, containing water slightly warmed and perfumed, are placed to each person at dessert. In these you may dip the tips of your fingers, wiping them afterwards on your table-napkin. If the finger-glass and doyley are placed on your dessert-plate, you should immediately remove the doyley to the left of your plate, and place the finger-glass upon it. By these means you leave the right for the wine-glasses.

Be careful to know the shapes of the various kinds of wine-glasses commonly in use, in order that you may never put forward one for another. High and narrow, and very broad and shallow glasses, are used for champagne; large, goblet-shaped glasses for burgundy and claret; ordinary wine-glasses for sherry and madeira; green glasses for hock; and somewhat large, bell-shaped glasses for port.

Port, sherry, and madeira are decanted. Hocks and champagnes appear in their native bottles. Claret and burgundy are handed around in a claret jug.

Coffee and liqueurs should be handed round when the dessert has been about a quarter of an hour on the table. After this, the ladies generally retire.

Should no servant be present to do so, the gentleman who is nearest the door should hold it for the ladies to pass through.

When the ladies are leaving the dining-room, the gentlemen all rise in their places, and do not resume their seats till the last lady is gone.

If you should unfortunately overturn or break anything, do not apologize for it. You can show your regret in your face, but it is not well-bred to put it into words.

Should you injure a lady's dress, apologize amply, and assist her, if possible, to remove all traces of the damage.

To abstain from taking the last piece on the dish, or the last glass of wine in the decanter, only because it is the last, is highly ill-bred. It implies a fear that the vacancy cannot be supplied, and almost conveys an affront to your host.

In summing up the little duties and laws of the table, a popular author has said that—" The chief matter of consideration at the dinner-table—as, indeed, everywhere else in the life of a gentleman—is to be perfectly composed and at his ease. He speaks deliberately; he performs the most important act of the day as if he were performing the most ordinary. Yet there is no appearance of trifling or want of gravity in his manner, he maintains the dignity which is so becoming on so vital an occasion. He performs all the ceremonies, yet in the style of one who who performs no ceremonies at all. He goes through all the complicated duties of the scene as if he were ' to the manner born.'"

To the giver of a dinner we have but one or two remarks to offer. If he be a bachelor, he had better give his dinner at a good hotel. If a married man, he will, we presume, enter into council with his wife and his cook. In any case, however, he should always bear in mind that it is his duty to entertain his friends in the best manner that his means permit; and that this is the least he can do to recompense them for the expenditure of time and money which they incur in accepting his invitation.

In conclusion, we may observe that to sit long in the dining-room after the ladies have retired is to pay a bad compliment to the hostess and her fair visitors; and that it is still worse to rejoin them with a flushed face and impaired powers of thought. A refined gentleman is always temperate.

I.—HOW TO ORGANIZE A DANCING PARTY OR BALL.

AS the number of guests at a dinner-party is regulated by the size of the table, so should the number of invitations to a ball be limited by the proportions of the dancing or ball-room. A prudent hostess will always invite a few more guests than she really desires to entertain, in the certainty that there will be some deserters when the appointed evening comes round; but she will at the same time remember that to overcrowd her room is to spoil the pleasure of those who love dancing, and that a party of this kind when too numerously attended is as great a failure as one at which too few are present.

A room which is nearly square, yet a little longer than it is broad, will be found the most favorable for a ball. It admits of two quadrille parties, or two round dances, at the same time. In a perfectly square room this arrangement is not so practicable or pleasant. A very long and narrow room, and their number in this country is legion, is obviously of the worst shape for the purpose of dancing, and is fit only for quadrilles and country dances.

The top of the ball room is the part nearest the musicians. In a private room, the top is where it would be if the room were a dining-room. It is generally at the farthest point from the door. Dancers should be careful to ascertain the top of the room before taking their places, as the top couples always lead the dances.

A good floor is of the first importance in a ball-room. In a private house, nothing can be better than a smooth, well-stretched holland, with the carpet beneath.

Abundance of light and free ventilation are indispensable to the spirits and comfort of the dancers.

Good music is as necessary to the prosperity of a ball as good wine to the excellence of a dinner. No hostess should tax her friends for this part of the entertainment. It is the most injurious economy imaginable. Ladies who would prefer to dance are tied to the pianoforte; and as few amateurs have been trained in the art of playing dance music, with that strict attention to time and accent which is absolutely necessary to the comfort of the dancers, a total and general discontent is sure to be the result. To play dance music thoroughly well is a branch of the art which requires considerable practice. It is as different from every other kind of playing as whale fishing is from fly fishing. Those who give private balls will do well ever to bear this in mind, and to provide skilled musicians for the evening. For a small party, a piano and cornopean make a very pleasant combination. Unless where several instruments are engaged we do not recommend the introduction of the violin; although in some respects the finest of all solo instruments, it is apt to sound thin and shrill when employed on mere inexpressive dance tunes, and played by a mere dance player.

Invitations to a ball or dance should be issued in the name of the lady of the house, and written on small note-paper of the best quality. Elegant printed forms, some of them printed in gold or silver, are to be had at every stationer's by those who prefer them. The paper may be gilt-edged, but not colored.

An invitation to a ball should be sent out at least ten days before the evening appointed. A fortnight, three weeks, and even a month may be allowed in the way of notice.

Not more than two or three days should be permitted to elapse before you reply to an invitation of this kind. The reply should always be addressed to the lady of the house, and should be couched in the same person as the invitation. The following are the forms generally in use:—

Mrs. Molyneux requests the honor of Captain Hamilton's company at an evening party, on Monday, March the 11th instant.
Dancing will begin at Nine o'clock.
Thursday, March 1st.

Captain Hamilton has much pleasure in accepting Mrs. Molyneux's polite invitation for Monday evening, March the 11th instant.
Friday, March 2d.

The old form of "presenting compliments" is now out of fashion.

If Mrs. Molyneux writes to Captain Hamilton in the first

person, as "My dear Sir," he is bound in etiquette to reply "My dear Madam."

The lady who gives a ball * should endeavor to secure an equal number of dancers of both sexes. Many private parties are spoiled by the preponderance of young ladies, some of whom never get partners at all, unless they dance with each other.

A room should in all cases be provided for the accommodation of the ladies. In this room there ought to be several looking-glasses; attendants to assist the fair visitors in the arrangement of their hair and dress; and some place in which the cloaks and shawls can be laid in order, and found at a moment's notice. It is well to affix tickets to the cloaks, giving a duplicate at the same time to each lady, as at the public theaters and concert rooms. Needles and thread should also be at hand, to repair any little accident incurred in dancing.

Another room should be devoted to refreshments, and kept amply supplied with coffee, lemonade, ices, wine, and biscuits during the evening. Where this cannot be arranged, the refreshments should be handed round between the dances.

The question of supper is one which so entirely depends on the means of those who give a ball or evening party, that very little can be said upon it in a treatise of this description. Where money is no object, it is of course always preferable to have the whole supper, "with all appliances and means to boot," sent in from some first-rate house. It spares all trouble whether to the entertainers or their servants, and relieves the hostess of every anxiety. Where circumstances render such a course imprudent, we would only observe that a home-provided supper, however simple, should be good of its kind, and abundant in quantity. Dancers are generally hungry people, and feel themselves much aggrieved if the supply of sandwiches proves unequal to the demand.

II.—BALL-ROOM TOILETTE.

LADIES.

The style of a lady's dress is a matter so entirely dependent on age, means, and fashion, that we can offer but little advice upon it. Fashion is so variable, that statements which are true of it to-day may be false a month hence. Respecting no institution of modern society is it so difficult to pronounce half-a-dozen permanent rules.

We may perhaps be permitted to suggest the following leading principles; but we do so with diffidence. Rich colors harmonize with rich brunette complexions and dark hair. Delicate colors are the most suitable for delicate and fragile styles of beauty. Very young ladies are never so suitably attired as in white. Ladies who dance should wear dresses of light and diaphanous materials, such as *tulle*, gauze, crape, net, etc., over colored silk slips. Silk dresses are not suitable for dancing. A married lady who dances only a few quadrilles may wear a *decolletée* silk dress with propriety.

Very stout persons should never wear white. It has the effect of adding to the bulk of the figure.

---

* It will be understood that we use the word "ball" to signify a private party where there is dancing, as well as a public ball.

Black and scarlet or black and violet are worn in mourning.

A lady in deep mourning should not dance at all.

However fashionable it may be to wear very long dresses, those ladies who go to a ball with the intention of dancing and enjoying the dance, should cause their dresses to be made short enough to clear the ground. We would ask them whether it is not better to accept this slight deviation from an absurd fashion, than to appear for three parts of the evening in a torn and pinned-up skirt.

Well-made shoes, whatever their color or material, and faultless gloves, are indispensable to the effect of a ball-room toilette.

Much jewelry is out of place in a ball-room. Beautiful flowers, whether natural or artificial, are the loveliest ornaments that a lady can wear on these occasions.

GENTLEMEN.

A black suit, thin enameled boots, a white neckcloth, and white or delicate gray gloves, are the chief points of a gentleman's ball-room toilette. He may wear a plain-bosomed shirt with one stud. White waistcoats are now fashionable. Much display of jewelry is no proof of good taste. A handsome watch-chain with, perhaps, the addition of a few costly trifles suspended to it, and a single shirt-stud, are the only adornments of this kind that a gentleman should wear.

A gentleman's dress is necessarily so simple that it admits of no compromise in point of quality and style. The material should be the best that money can procure, and the fashion unexceptionable. So much of the outward man depends on his tailor, that we would urge no gentleman to economize in this matter.

ETIQUETTE OF THE BALL-ROOM.

On entering the ball-room, the visitor should at once seek the lady of the house, and pay his respects to her. Having done this, he may exchange salutations with such friends and acquaintances as may be in the room.

If the ball be a public one, and a gentleman desires to dance with any lady to whom he is a stranger, he must apply to a member of the floor committee for an introduction.

Even in private balls, no gentleman can invite a lady to dance without a previous introduction. This introduction should be effected through the lady of the house or a member of her family.

No lady should accept an invitation to dance from a gentleman to whom she has not been introduced. In case any gentleman should commit the error of so inviting her, she should not excuse herself on the plea of a previous engagement or of fatigue, as to do so would imply that she did not herself attach due importance to the necessary ceremony of introduction. Her best reply would be to the effect that she would have much pleasure in accepting his invitation if he would procure an introduction to her. This observation may be taken as applying only to public balls. At a private party the host and hostess are sufficient guarantees for the respectability of their guests; and although a gentleman would show a singular want of knowledge of the laws of society in acting as we have supposed, the lady who should reply to him as if he were merely an impertinent stranger in a public assembly-room would be implying an affront to her entertainers. The mere fact of being assembled together under the roof of a mutual friend, is in itself a kind of general introduction of the guests to each other.

An introduction given for the mere purpose of enabling a lady and gentleman to go through a dance together does not constitute an acquaintanceship. The lady is at liberty, should she feel like doing so, to pass the gentleman the next day without recognition.

To attempt to dance without a knowledge of dancing is not only to make one's self ridiculous, but one's partner also. No lady or gentleman has a right to place a partner in this absurd position.

Never forget a ball-room engagement. To do so is to commit an unpardonable offense against good breeding.

It is not necessary that a lady or gentleman should be acquainted with the *steps* in order to walk gracefully and easily through a quadrille. An easy carriage and a knowledge of the figure is all that is requisite. A round dance, however, should on no account be attempted without a thorough knowledge of the steps and some previous practice.

No person who has not a good ear for time and tune need hope to dance well.

At the conclusion of a dance the gentleman bows to his partner, and either promenades with her round the room or takes her to a seat. Where a room is set apart for refreshments he offers to conduct her thither. At a public ball no gentleman would, of course, permit a lady to pay for refreshments. Good taste forbids that a lady and gentleman should dance too frequently together at either a public or private ball. Engaged persons should be careful not to commit this conspicuous solecism.

If a lady happens to forget a previous engagement, and stands up with another partner, the gentleman whom she has thus slighted is bound to believe that she has acted from mere inadvertence, and should by no means suffer his pride to master his good temper. To cause a disagreeable scene in a private ball-room is to affront your host and hostess, and to make yourself absurd. In a public room it is no less reprehensible.

Always remember that good breeding and good temper (or the appearance of good temper) are inseparably connected.

Young gentlemen are earnestly advised not to limit their conversation to remarks on the weather and the heat of the room. It is to a certain extent incumbent on them to do something more than dance when they invite a lady to join a quadrille. If it be only upon the news of the day, a gentleman should be able to afford at least three or four observations to his partner in the course of a long half hour.

Gentlemen who dance cannot be too careful not to injure the dresses of the ladies who do them the honor to stand up with them. The young men of the present day are singularly careless in this respect, and when they have torn a lady's delicate skirt appear to think the mischief they have done scarcely worth the trouble of an apology.

A gentleman conducts his last partner to the supper-room, and having waited upon her while there, re-conducts her to the ball-room.

Never attempt to take a place in a dance which has been previously engaged.

A thoughtful hostess will never introduce a bad dancer to a good one, because she has no right to punish one friend in order to oblige another.

It is not customary for married persons to dance together in society.

IV.—THE QUADRILLE.

The Quadrille is the most universal, as it is certainly the most sociable of all fashionable dances. It admits of pleasant conversation, frequent interchange of partners, and is adapted to every age, the young or old; the ponderous *paterfamilias* or his sylph-like daughter, may with equal propriety take part in its easy and elegant figures. Even an occasional blunder is of less consequence in this dance than in many others, for each personage is in some degree free as to his own movements, not being compelled by the continual embrace of his partner to dance either better or worse than he may find convenient.

People now generally walk through a quadrille. Nothing more than a perfect knowledge of the figure, a graceful demeanor, and a correct ear for the time of the music are requisite to enable any one to take a creditable part in this dance.

As soon as a gentleman has engaged his partner for the quadrille, he should endeavor to secure as his *vis-à-vis* some friend or acquaintance and should then lead his partner to the top of the quadrille, provided that post of honor be still vacant. He will place the lady always at his right hand.

Quadrille music is divided into eight bars for each part of the figure; two steps should be taken in every bar; every movement thus invariably consists of eight or four steps.

It is well not to learn too many new figures: the memory is liable to become confused among them; besides which, it is doubtful whether your partner, or your *vis-à-vis*, is as learned in the matter as yourself. Masters are extremely fond of inventing and teaching new figures; but you will do well to confine your attention to a few simple and universally received sets, which you will find quite sufficient for your purpose. We begin with the oldest and most common, the

FIRST SET OF QUADRILLES.

First Figure.—Le Pantalon.

The couples at the top and bottom of the quadrille cross to each other's places in eight steps, occupying four bars of the time; re-cross immediately to their own places, which completes the movement of eight bars. This is called the *Chaine Anglaise*. The gentleman always keeps to the right of *vis-à-vis* lady in crossing, thus placing her *inside*.

Set to partners, or *balancez;* turn your partners. (This occupies the second eight bars.) Ladies chain, or *chaine des dames*. (Eight bars more.) Each couple crosses to opposite couple's place, gentleman giving his hand to his partner: this is called half-promenade. Couples recross right and left to their places, without giving hands, which completes another eight bars, and ends the figure.

The side couples repeat what the top and bottom couples have done.

Second Figure.—L'Eté.

The ladies in all the top couples, and their *vis-à-vis* gentlemen, advance four steps, and retire the same, repeating this movement once again, which makes the first eight bars.

Top ladies and *vis-à-vis* gentlemen cross to each other's places; advance four steps; retreat ditto; cross back towards partners, who set to them as they advance; turn partners, which ends first half of figure.

Second ladies and top *vis-à-vis* gentlemen execute the same movements. Then side couples begin, the privilege of commencement being conferred on those ladies who stand at the *right* of the top couples.

This figure is sometimes performed in a different manner, known as double *L'Eté*. Instead of the top lady and *vis-à-vis* gentleman advancing alone, they advance with partners, joining hands; cross and return, as in the single figure. This variation is, however, somewhat out of vogue, except (as will presently be seen) in the last figure of the quadrille, where it is still frequently introduced.

Third Figure.—La Poule.

Top lady and *vis-à-vis* gentleman cross to each other's places, giving right hand in passing; cross back again with left hand. (Eight bars.) The two couples form in a line, and join hands, the left hand of one holding the right hand of his or her neighbor, so that each faces different ways; in this position all four *balancez*, then half promenade with partner to opposite place: top lady and *vis-à-vis* gentleman advance four steps and retire ditto. (2d eight bars.) Both top and bottom couples advance together, and retire the same; then re-cross right and left to places. (3d eight bars.) Second lady and first opposite gentleman repeat figure. Side couples repeat, observing same rule for commencement as in *L'Eté*.

Fourth Figure.—La Trenise.

Top couples join hands, advance four steps and retreat ditto; advance again, gentleman leaving lady at left hand of *vis-à-vis* gentleman, and retiring alone. (1st eight bars.) Two ladies advance, crossing to opposite side; gentleman advances to meet his partner, *vis-à-vis* lady returns to hers. (2d eight bars.) *Balancez;* turns partners to places. (3d eight bars.) Second couple performs same figure; side couples repeat as before.

If *La Pastorale* be preferred, it will be performed thus:— Top couples advance and retreat; advance, gentleman leading lady to left hand of *vis-à-vis* gentleman; he advances with both ladies four steps, retreating ditto; again advancing he leaves both ladies with first gentleman, retreating alone; top gentleman and both ladies advance and retreat; again advance, joining hands in circle, go half round, half promenade to opposite places, then return right and left to their own. Second couples and side couples repeat as before.

Fifth Figure.—La Finale.

Begin with the *grand rond* or great round; that is, the whole quadrille; first and second couples and sides join hands all around, advance four steps, and retreat ditto. *L'Eté* is now sometimes introduced, the *grand rond* being repeated between each division of the figure. But it gives a greater variety and *brio* to the quadrille if, after the first *grand rond*, the following figure be performed, the *galop* step being used throughout. Each gentleman (at top and bottom couples) takes his lady round the waist, as for the *galop;* advance four steps, retreat ditto, advance again, cross to opposite places; advance, retreat, re-cross to own places. Ladies chain; half promenade across; half right and left to places; *grand rond*. Side couples repeat figure. *Grand rond* between each division and at the conclusion. Bow to your partners, and conduct your lady to seat.

V.—THE LANCERS.

The Lancers Quadrille is perhaps the most graceful and animated of any. Within the last few years it has become a great favorite in fashionable circles. It admits of much skill and elegance in executing its quick and varied figures, a correct acquaintance with which is absolutely requisite to all who take part in it. Unlike the common quadrille, the Lancers must be danced by four couples only in each set; though of course there can be many sets dancing at the same time. The number being so limited, one awkward or ignorant person confuses the whole set; therefore, it is indispensable that every one who dances in this quadrille should have a thorough mastery of its graceful intricacies. We have observed that of late it has become the fashion to substitute new tunes and new figures for the old well-known music of the Lancers Quadrille. We cannot consider this an improvement. The old simple melodies are peculiarly fitted to the sprightly, joyous character of the dance; which is more than can be said for any of the modern substitutes. When these are used, the Lancers, in our opinion, loses its individuality and spirit, becoming almost like a common quadrille. We should be heartily glad to see the old tunes restored, once for all, to their rightful supremacy.

The sets of four couples, top, opposite, and sides, having been arranged, the dance begins as follows:—

1st Figure.—First lady and opposite gentleman advance and retreat; advance again, joining their hands; pass round each other and back to places. (1st eight bars.) Top couple join hands, and cross, opposite couple crossing at the same time, separately, outside them; the same reversed, back to places. (2d eight bars.) All the couples *balancez* to corners; each gentleman turns his neighbor's partner back to places. (3d eight bars.) Second couple repeat figure from beginning; after them side couples, those who stand to the right of top couple having always the priority, as in the common quadrille.

2d Figure.—First couple advance and retreat, gentleman holding lady's left hand; advance again; gentleman leaves his partner in the center of the quadrille, and retires to place. (1st eight bars.) *Balancez* to each other and turn to places. (2d eight bars.) Side couples join first and second couples, forming a line of four on either side. Each line advances four steps, retreats ditto; then advances again, each gentleman reclaiming his partner, and all turn to places. Second and side couples repeat figure in succession.

3d Figure.—First lady advances four steps alone, and stops; *vis-à-vis* gentleman does the same; first lady retires, facing gentleman, to whom she makes a slow profound courtesy. (The courtesy must occupy a bar or two of the music; and as, if made with grace and dignity, it is most effective, we would recommend ladies to practice it carefully beforehand.) The gentleman at the same time bows and retires (1st eight bars). All four ladies advance to center, give right hands across to each other (which is called the *double chain*), and left hand to *vis-à-vis* gentleman; then back again, left hands across in the middle, and right hands to partners back to places. (2d eight bars.) Second and side couples repeat figure from commencement.

A more recent fashion for dancing this figure is as follows: Instead of one lady advancing at first, all four advance, and courtesy to each other; then turn and courtesy to their partners. Ladies do the *moulinet* in the center; that is, give right hands across to each other, and half round; left hands across back again, and return to places. Gentlemen meantime all move round outside the ladies, till each has regained his place. Figure as usual repeated four times; but the second and fourth time the gentlemen advance instead of the ladies, and bow, first to each other, then to their partners; continuing as before through the rest of the figure.

4th Figure.—Top gentleman, taking partner's left hand, leads her to the couple on their right, to whom they bow and courtesy (which civility must be met with the like acknowledgment), then cross quickly to fourth couple, and do the same. (1st eight bars.) All four couples *chassez croisez* right and left (gentleman invariably passing behind his partner), then turn hands (*tour des mains*) back to places. (2d eight bars.) First and opposite couples right and left across and back again to places. (3d eight bars.) Second and sides repeat as usual.

5th Figure.—This figure commences with the music. Each couple should stand ready, the gentleman facing his partner, his right hand holding hers. If every one does not start directly the music begins, and does not observe strict time throughout, this somewhat intricate figure becomes hopelessly embarrassed; but, when well danced, it is the prettiest of the set. It commences with the *grande chaine* all round; each gentleman giving his right hand to his partner at starting, his left to the next lady, then his right again, and so all round, till all have returned to their places. (This occupies sixteen bars of the music.) First couple promenade inside figure, returning to places with their backs turned to opposite couple. The side couple on their right falls in immediately behind them; the fourth couple follows, the second couple remaining in their places. A double line is thus formed—ladies on one side and gentlemen on the other. (3d eight bars.) All *chassez croisez*, ladies left, gentlemen right, behind partners. First lady leads off, turning sharply round to the right; first gentleman does the same to the left, meeting at the bottom of the quadrille, and promenade back to places. All the ladies follow first lady; all the gentlemen follow first gentleman; and as each meets his partner at the bottom of the figure, they touch hands, then fall back in two lines—ladies on one side, gentlemen on the other—facing each other. (4th eight bars.) Four ladies join hands, advance, and retreat; four gentlemen ditto at the same time; then each turns his partner to places. (5th eight bars.) *Grande chaine* again. Second and side couples repeat the whole figure in succession, each couple taking its turn to lead off, as the first had done. *Grande chaine* between each figure and in conclusion.

VI.—THE LANCERS FOR SIXTEEN, OR DOUBLE LANCERS.

1st Figure.—Two first ladies and *vis-à-vis* gentlemen begin at the same moment, and go through the figure as in Single Lancers. All *balancez* to corners; in other words, each lady sets to gentlemen at her right, who turns her to her place. Second couples and sides repeat as usual.

2d Figure.—First couples advance, retreat, advance again, leaving ladies in center; set to partners and turn to places. Two side couples nearest first couples join them; two side couples nearest second couples do the same, thus forming eight in each line. They all advance and retreat, holding hands, then turn partners to places. Repeated by second and side couples as usual.

3d Figure.—First ladies advance and stop; *vis-à-vis* gentlemen ditto; courtesy profoundly, bow, and back to places. Ladies do the *moulinet*, gentlemen go round outside, and back to places. Or, ladies advance and courtesy to each other and then to partners; gentlemen doing the same when the second and fourth couples begin the figure, as in Single Lancers.

4th Figure.—First couples advance to couples on their right; bow and courtesy; cross to opposite side, bow and courtesy, *chassez croisez*, and return to place. Right and left to opposite places, and back again. Second couples and sides repeat figure.

5th Figure.—*Grande chaine* all round, pausing at the end of every eight bars to bow and courtesy; continue *chaine* back to places, which will occupy altogether thirty-two bars of the music. Figure almost the same as in Single Lancers. Both first couples lead around, side couples falling in behind, thus forming four sets of lines. Figure repeated by second and side couples; *grande chaine* between each figure and at the conclusion.

VII. DOUBLE QUADRILLE.

This quadrille contains the same figures as the common quadrille, but so arranged that they are danced by four instead of two couples. All quadrille music suits it; and it occupies just half the time of the old quadrille. It makes an agreeable variety in the movements of the dance, and is easily learned. It requires four couples.

First Figure.—Pantalon.

First and second couples right and left, whilst side couples dance the *chaine Anglaise* outside them. All four couples set to partners and turn them. Four ladies form ladies' chain, or hands across in the middle of the figure, giving first right hands, and then left, back to places. Half promenade, first and second couples do *chaine Anglaise*, while side couples do *grande chaine* round them. This leaves all in their right places, and ends figure.

Second Figure.—L'Été.

First lady, and lady on her right hand, perform the figure with their *vis-à-vis* gentlemen, as in common *L'Été*; taking care, when they cross, to make a semi-circle to the left. Second couple and second side couple repeat figure, as in common *L'Été*.

Third Figure.—La Poule.

Top lady and *vis-à-vis* gentleman, lady at her right, and her opposite gentleman, perform figure at the same time, setting to each other in two cross lines. Other couples follow as usual.

Fourth Figure.—La Pastorale.

The first and opposite couples dance the figure, not with each other, but with the couples to their right. The latter do the same with first and second couples.

Fifth Figure.—Finale.

Galopade all round. Top and opposite couples galopade forwards, and retreat. As they retreat side couples advance; and, as they retreat in their turn, first and second couples galopade to each others places. Side couples the same. First and second couples advance again; side couples the same as the others retreat; first and second back to places as side couples retreat. Side couples back to places. Double *chaine des dames*, and galopade all round. Then side couples repeat figure as usual, and *galop* all round in conclusion.

It is requisite to keep correct time and step in this quadrille, which would otherwise become much confused.

VIII. THE POLKA.

The origin of this once celebrated dance is difficult to ascertain. It is believed by some to be of great antiquity, and to have been brought into Germany from the East. Others affirm that its origin is of more recent date, and its birthplace considerably nearer home. An authority on these matters remarks: "In spite of what those professors say who proclaim themselves to have learned the Polka in Germany, or as being indebted for it to an Hungarian nobleman, we are far from placing confidence in their assertions. In our opinion Paris is its birthplace, and its true author, undoubtedly, the now far-famed Monsieur Cellarius, for whom this offspring of his genius has gained a European celebrity."

Whatever we may be inclined to believe with regard to this disputed question, there can be no doubt of the wide-spread popularity which for many years was enjoyed by the Polka. When first introduced in 1843, it was received with enthusiasm; and it effected a complete revolution in the style of dancing which had prevailed up to that period. A brisk, lively character was imparted even to the steady-going quadrille; the old *Valse à Trois Temps* was pronounced insufferably "slow"; and its brilliant rival, the *Valse à Deux Temps*, which had been recently introduced, at once established the supremacy which it has ever since maintained. The *galop*, which had been until this period only an occasional dance, now assumed a prominent post in every ball-room, dividing the honors with the valse.

Perhaps no dance affords greater facilities for the display of ignorance or skill, elegance or vulgarity, than the Polka. The step is simple and easily acquired, but the method of dancing it varies *ad infinitum*. Some persons race and romp through the dance in a manner fatiguing to themselves and dangerous to their fellow-dancers. Others (though this is more rare) drag their partner listlessly along, with a sovereign contempt alike for the requirements of the time and the spirit of the music. Some gentlemen hold their partner so tight that she is half suffocated; others hold her so loosely that she continually slips away from them. All these extremes are equally objectionable, and defeat the graceful intention of the dance. It should be performed quietly, but with spirit, and *always in strict time*. The head and shoulders should be kept still, not jerked and turned at every step, as is the manner of some. The feet should glide swiftly along the floor—not hopping or jumping as if the boards were red-hot.

You should clasp your partner lightly but firmly round the waist with your right arm.

Your left hand takes her right hand; but beware of elevating your arm and hers in the air, or holding them out straight, which suggests the idea of windmills.

Above all, never place your left hand on your hip or behind you. In the first place, you thus drag your partner too much forward, which makes her look ungraceful; in the next, this attitude is *never used* except in casinos, and it is almost an insult to introduce it in a respectable ball-room.

Let the hand which clasps your partner's fall easily by your side in a natural position, and keep it there. Your partner's left hand rests on your right shoulder; her right arm is thrown a little forwards toward your left.

The Polka is danced in $\frac{2}{4}$ time. There are three steps in each bar; the fourth beat is always a rest.

It is next to impossible to describe in words the step of the Polka, or of any circular dance: nothing but example can correctly teach it; and although we shall do our best to be as clear as possible, we would earnestly recommend those of our readers who desire to excel, whether in this or the following dances, to take a few lessons from some competent instructor.

The gentleman starts with his left foot, the lady with her right. We shall describe the step as danced by the gentleman; the same directions, reversing the order of the feet, will apply to the lady.

1st beat.—Spring slightly on right foot, at the same time slide left foot forward.

2d beat.—Bring right foot forward by *glissade*, at the same time raising left foot.

3d beat.—Bring left foot slightly forward and *fall* upon it, leaving right foot raised, and the knee slightly bent, ready to begin the step at the first beat of the next bar.

4th beat.—Remain on left foot. Begin next bar with the right foot, and repeat the step to end of third beat. Begin the following bar with left foot, and so on; commencing each bar with right or left foot alternately.

The Polka is danced with a circular movement, like the Valse; in each bar you half turn, so that by the end of the second bar, you have brought your partner completely round.

The circular movement of the Polka admits of two directions—from right or left or from left to right. The ordinary direction is from right to left. The opposite one is known as the *reverse* step. It is more difficult to execute, but is a pleasant change for skilled dancers, if they have become giddy from turning too long in one direction.

In dancing the Polka, or any circular dance where a large number of couples are performing at the same time, the gentleman must be careful to steer his fair burden safely through the mazes of the crowded ball-room. A little watchfulness can almost always avoid collisions, and a good dancer would consider himself disgraced if any mishap occurred to a lady under his care. Keep a sharp lookout, and avoid crowded corners. Should so many couples be dancing as to render such caution impossible, stop at once and do not go on until the room has become somewhat cleared. In a few minutes others will have paused to rest, and you can then continue. Your partner will be grateful that your consideration has preserved her from the dismal plight in which we have seen some ladies emerge from this dance—their *coiffeurs* disordered, their dresses torn, and their cheeks crimson with fatigue and mortification, while their indignant glances plainly showed the anger they did not care to express in words, and which their reckless partner had fully deserved. A torn dress is sometimes not the heaviest penalty incurred : we have known more than one instance where ladies have been lamed for weeks through the culpable carelessness of their partners; their tender feet having been half crushed beneath some heavy boot in one of these awkward collisions. This is a severe price to pay for an evening's amusement, and gentlemen are bound to be cautious how they inflict it or anything approaching to it, upon their fair companions. Ladies, on the other hand will do well to remember that by leaning heavily upon their partner's shoulder, dragging back from his encircling arm, or otherwise impeding the freedom of his movements, they materially add to his labor and take from his pleasure in the dance. They should endeavor to lean as lightly, and give as little trouble as possible; for, however flattering to the vanity of the nobler sex may be the idea of feminine dependence, we question whether the reality, in the shape of a dead weight upon their aching arms throughout a Polka or a Valse of twenty minutes' duration, would be acceptable to even the most chivalrous among them.

We have been thus minute in our instructions, because they not only apply to the Polka, but equally to all circular dances where a great number stand up to dance at the same time. We now pass on to the Mazourka.

The time of the Mazourka is ¾, like the common valse; but it should be played much more slowly; if danced quickly, it becomes an unmeaning succession of hops, and its graceful character is destroyed.

We describe the step as danced by the lady; for the gengentleman it will be the same, with the feet reversed; that is, for right foot read left, and so on.

First Step.

1st and 2d beats.—Spring on left foot, sliding forward right foot at the same time, and immediately let your weight rest on the forward foot. This occupies two beats.

3d beat.—Spring on right foot; this ends the bar.

2d bar, 1st and 2d beats.—Spring again on right foot, and slide forward left at same time. Rest on it a moment as before during second beat; at third beat spring on it; which ends second bar. Continue same step throughout. You will perceive that, at the first and third beats of the time, you hop slightly, resting, during the second beats, on the foremost foot.

Second Step.

1st beat.—Spring on left foot, slightly striking both heels together.

2d beat.—Slide right foot to the right, bending the knee.

3d beat.—Bring the left foot up to right foot with a slight spring, raising right foot; which ends the first bar.

2d bar, 1st beat.—Spring again on left foot, striking it with heel of right.

2d beat.—Slide right foot to the right.

3d beat.—Fall on right foot, raising left foot behind it, which ends the second bar. Reverse the step by springing first on the right foot, and sliding the left, etc. The music generally indicates that this step should be repeated three times to the right, which occupies three bars then *rest* during the fourth bar, and return with reverse step to the left during the three bars which follow, resting again at the eighth bar.

Third Step.

1st beat.—Spring on left foot, and slide right foot to the right.

2d beat.—Rest on right foot.

3d beat.—Spring on right foot, bringing left foot up behind it.

2d bar, 1st beat.—Spring on right foot, sliding left foot to the left.

2d beat.—Rest on left foot.

3d beat.—Hop on left foot, bringing right behind as before. Continue at pleasure.

The first of these three steps is most commonly used in the valse; but the second is an agreeable change for those who may have grown giddy or weary in doing the *figure en tournant* (circular movement).

Be careful not to exaggerate the slight hop at the first and third beats of each bar; and to *slide* the foot gracefully forward, not merely to make a step, as some bad dancers do.

IX. THE MAZOURKA QUADRILLE.

This elegant quadrille has five figures, and can be performed by any even number of couples. The music, like the step, is that of the Mazourka. The couples are arranged as in the ordinary quadrille.

Join hands all round; *grand rond* to the left (four bars), then back again to the right (four bars), employing the *second* step of the Mazourka. Each couple does the *petit tour* forwards and backwards, still using the second step, and repeating it three times to the right—then resting a bar; three times to the left—then resting another bar; which occupies eight bars of the music. These figures may be considered as preliminary.

1st Figure.—Top and bottom couples right and left (eight

bars), with Redowa step;* then they advance, the ladies cross over, the gentlemen meanwhile pass quickly round each other, and return to own places (four bars); *petit tour* forward with opposite ladies (four bars); right and left (eight bars); advance again; the ladies return to own places, and the gentlemen pass again round each other to their own ladies (four bars; *petit tour* backward (four bars). Side couples do likewise.

2d Figure. — (Eight bars rest). Top and bottom couples advance and retire, hands joined (four bars). All cross over into opposite places, each going to each other's left (four bars); *petit tour* forward (four bars); advance and retire (four bars), and return to places (four bars); *petit tour* (four bars). Side couples do likewise.

3d Figure. — (Eight bars rest.) Top and bottom ladies cross over into opposite places (four bars); return, presenting left hand to each other, and right hand to partner, as in *La Poule* (four bars); pass round with partners into opposite places (four bars); *petit tour* backward (four bars); *vis-à-vis* couples hands across, round (six bars); retire (two bars); top and bottom ladies cross over (four bars); ladies cross again, giving each other left hands, and right to partners (four bars). All pass round to own places (four bars); *petit tour* backward (four bars).

4th Figure. — (Eight bars rest.) Top couple lead round inside the figure (eight bars); *petit tour* forward and backward (eight bars); advance to opposite couple; the gentleman turns half round without quitting his partner, and gives his left hand to opposite lady; the two ladies join hands behind gentleman (four bars); in this position the three advance and retire (eight bars). The gentleman passes under the ladies' arms; all three pass round to the left, with second step of Mazourka, the opposite lady finishing in her own place (four bars). The top couple return to places (four bars); *petit tour* forward (four bars). Opposite couple and side couples do likewise.

5th Figure. — (Eight bars rest.) Top and bottom couples half right and left (four bars); *petit tour* backward (four bars); half right and left to places (four bars); *petit tour* backward (four bars); *vis-à-vis* couples hands round to opposite places (four bars); *petit tour* forward (four bars); hands round to own places (four bars); *petit tour* (four bars); right and left (eight bars).

Side couples do likewise.

Finale. — Grand round all to the left, and then to the right (sixteen bars); grand chain, as in the Lancers, with first step of Mazourka (sixteen bars). But if there are more than eight in the quadrille, the music must be continued until all have regained their places.

N.B. — Music continues during rests.

X. — THE POLKA MAZOURKA.

The step of this dance is, as its name implies, a mixture of the steps of the Polka and the Mazourka. The time is ⅜ quicker than that of the Mazourka.

Gentleman takes his partner as in the valse. *Figure en*

---

* This step will be found farther on under the head of Redowa Valse.

tournant. We describe the steps for the gentleman; the lady simply reverses the order of the feet, using left foot for right throughout.

1st beat. — Rest on right foot, with left foot a little raised behind, and slide left foot to the left.

2d beat. — Spring on the right foot, bringing it up to where left foot is, and raising the latter in front.

3d beat. — Spring once more on right foot, passing left foot behind without touching the ground with it; this ends first bar.

2d bar, 1st beat. — Slide left foot to the left, as before.

2d beat. — Spring on right foot, as before, and bring it up to the place of left foot, raising latter at same moment.

3d beat. — Fall on the left foot, and raise the right foot behind; end of second bar.

Begin third bar with right foot, and continue as before. You turn half round in the first three beats, and complete the circle in the second three.

XI — THE REDOWA, OR REDOVA.

The step of this valse somewhat resembles that of the Mazourka, and is used, as we have seen, in dancing the Mazourka Quadrille. It is an elegant valse, not so lively as the Polka Mazourka, but, if danced in correct time, not too slowly, is very graceful and pleasing. The step is not so difficult as that of the Mazourka: it is almost a *Pas de Basque*, with the addition of the hop. In all these dances, which partake of the nature of the Mazourka, it is requisite to mark distinctly the first and third beats of every bar, otherwise the peculiar character of the movement is completely lost. We describe the step for the lady as it is employed in the forward movement.

1st beat. — Stand with right foot slightly forward; spring upon it, bringing it behind left foot, which is raised at same time.

2d beat. — Slide your left foot forward, bending the knee.

3d beat. — Bring your right foot, with a slight hop, up behind your left foot, raising the latter and keeping it in front. (One bar.)

1st beat. — Spring upon your left foot, passing it behind your right, and raising latter.

2d beat. — Slide right foot forward, bending the knee.

3d beat. — Bring left foot up to right, with slight hop, and raise right foot at same moment, keeping it in front as before.

When the *figure en tournant* (circular movement) is employed, the lady begins by sliding the left foot forward, and the right foot backward. Gentleman always does the same, with order of feet reversed.

This dance has been very popular in Paris: in England it is now seldom seen.

XII. — THE SCHOTTISCHE.

The Schottische was introduced about the same time as the Polka Mazourka. Its origin is as uncertain as that of the Polka, and it is believed to be a very ancient national dance. It is a great favorite with the German peasantry; and although its name, *Schottische*, would seem to imply that it came form

Scotland, there is no doubt that it is essentially German alike in character and in music.

The step, although easy to learn, requires great precision. We would recommend our readers to adhere throughout to the circular movement. Some dancers begin by four steps to the right, then back again, not turning until they commence the second half of the figure. But when many couples are dancing this practice involves a risk of collisions, and it is safer to begin at once with the *figure en tournant*. The second part of the step consists of a series of slight hops, which must be made exactly at the same moment by both parties, otherwise a break-down is inevitable. They should be executed as quickly as possible, so as to avoid the *jigging* effect which bad dancers impart to the Schottische. When well performed it is a very animated and elegant dance, forming an agreeable variety to the Polka and Valse.

The time is $\frac{2}{4}$; it should be played a good deal slower than the Polka; when hurried it becomes ungraceful and vulgar. The first and third beat in each bar should be slightly marked.

We proceed to describe the step as danced by the gentleman.

Slide the left foot forward; bring right foot close behind left foot. Slide left foot forward a second time. Spring upon left foot. Then do the same with right foot.

Having completed four steps, first with the left foot, and then with the right, you come to the second part, which consists of a series of double hops, two on each foot alternately. Hop twice on the left foot (one hop for each beat of time), and half turn round; then twice on the right, completing the circular movement. Repeat the same through another four beats; then resume first step through the next two bars, and continue to alternate them every second bar. You can also vary the dance at pleasure, by continuing the first step without changing it for the hops; or you can likewise continue these throughout several bars in succession; taking care, of course, to appraise your partner of your intention. Even when well and quietly danced, there is something undignified in the hopping movement of the second step; and we have observed with satisfaction that for some time past it has been replaced by the step of the *Valse à Deux Temps*, which is now generally used instead of the double hops.

XIII.—LA VARSOVIENNE.

This is a round dance for two, which, like the Polka Mazourka, is a combination of the steps of one or two other dances. Since the introduction of the Polka and the Mazourka, several dances have been invented which partake largely of the character of both. La Varsovienne is very graceful. It is not often danced now.

Take your partner as for the valse. Count three in each bar. Time much the same as in Polka Mazourka. The music is generally divided into parts of sixteen bars each. The step for the gentleman is as follows in the first part:—

Slide left foot to the left; slightly spring forward with right foot, twice, leaving the left foot raised behind, in readiness for next step. (1st bar.) Repeat the same. (2d bar.) One polka step, during which turn. (3d bar.) Bring your right foot to the second position, and wait a whole bar. (4th bar.) Resume first step with right foot, and repeat throughout, reversing order of feet. Lady, as usual, begins with her right foot, doing the same step.

Second step in second part. 1st bar.—Gentleman, beginning with his left foot, does one polka step to the left, turning partner.

2d bar.—Bring right foot to the second position, and bend towards it; wait a whole bar.

3d bar.—One polka step with right foot to the right, turning partner.

4th bar.—Left foot to second position; bend towards it, and wait as before.

Third part.—Take three polka steps to the left. (This occupies three bars.) Bring right foot to second position, and wait one bar. Repeat the same, beginning with right foot to the right.

XIV.—THE GORLITZA.

This is a Polish round dance for two. Like the Varsovienne, it is now seldom seen beyond the walls of the dancing academy. Perhaps one reason of its short-lived popularity is to be found in the fact that it is rather troublesome to learn, the steps being changed continually. The time is the same as the Schottische, but not quite so quick. Take your position as for the Polka.

1st bar.—One polka step to the left, beginning with left foot, and turning half round.

2d bar.—Slide your right foot to right; bring left foot up close behind it, as in the fifth position; make a *glissade* with your right foot, ending with your left in front.

3d bar.—Spring on your right foot, raising your left in front. Fall on your left foot, passing it behind your right foot. *Glissade* right with right foot, ending with left in front.

4th bar.—Again spring on right foot, raising left in front. Fall on left foot, passing it behind right. *Glissade* to right, with your right foot; end with same foot in front. Then repeat from beginning during the next four bars, but the second time be careful to end with the left foot in front. During the last two bars you turn round, but do not move forward.

The step for the lady is the same, with the order of the feet, as usual, reversed; except, however, in the last two bars of this figure, which both begin with the same foot.

The Gorlitza, like the preceding dance, is divided into parts. The first part occupies eight bars of the music; the second sixteen bars. The step for the second part is as follows:—

1st four bars.—Commence with Polka Mazourka step, with left foot to the left, and turn half round. Then do the step of Mazourka to the right, beginning with the right foot. Fall on left foot, keeping it behind right foot; *glissade* with right foot, and end with same in front.

2d four bars.—Polka Mazourka with right foot to the right, and turn half round. Mazourka step with left foot to the left. Fall on right foot, keeping it behind; *glissade* with left foot, bringing it behind.

Repeat from beginning, which completes the sixteen bars of second half of the figure.

Lady does the same steps, with order of feet reversed.

XV.—THE VALSE A TROIS TEMPS.

Forty years ago, the Valse (or as it was then pronounced, *Waltz*) was a stately measure, danced with gravity and deliberation. Each couple wheeled round and round with dignified composure, never interrupting the monotony of the dance by any movements forward or backward. They consequently soon became giddy, although the music was not played above half as fast as the valse music of our day. We are bound to admit that this stately fashion of waltzing was infinitely more graceful than the style which has superseded it. But having confessed so much, we may venture to add that Valse, as danced by the present generation, possesses a spirit, lightness, and variety quite unknown to its stately predecessor.

Although we cannot regret the introduction of a more animated style of dancing, we are sorry that the old Waltz has been so entirely given up. When restored to its original *temps*, the *Valse à Trois Temps* is nearly as spirited as the *Valse à Deux*; and twice as graceful. It has the additional advantage over the latter, that it contains in each bar three steps to three beats of the time; whereas the *Deux Temps*, as its name implies, numbers only two steps in a bar of three notes; and is thus incorrect in time. We venture to predict that the old Waltz will, at no distant day, be restored to public favor.

Gentleman takes his partner round the waist with his right arm; his left hand holds hers, as in the Polka. Lady places left hand on his shoulder, and right hand in his left hand. Begin at once with the *figure en tournant*. Time ¾; one step to each beat. First beat in each bar should be slightly marked by the dancers.

1st beat.—Slide left foot backwards, towards the left.

2d beat.—Slide your right foot past your left in same direction, keeping right foot behind left, and turning slightly to the right.

3d beat.—Bring left foot up behind right (one bar).

1st beat.—Slide right foot forward toward the right.

2d beat.—Slide left foot forward, still turning towards right.

3d beat.—Bring right foot up to right, turning on both feet, so as to complete the circle (two bars). Remember to finish with right foot in front. Repeat from first beat of first bar. Gentleman always turns from left to right; lady from right to left.

The step of the old Waltz is simple enough; nevertheless some practice is required to dance it really well. Remember always to *slide*, not to *step*, forward; for the beauty of this valse consists in its gliding motion. It is not at first easy to dance swiftly and quietly at the same time; but a little patience will soon enable you to conquer that difficulty, and to do full justice to what is, in our opinion, the most perfectly graceful of all the round dances, without a single exception.

XVI. THE VALSE A DEUX TEMPS.

We are indebted to the mirth-loving capital of Austria for this brilliant Valse.

This Valse is incorrect in time. Two steps can never properly be made to occupy the space of three beats in the music. The ear requires that each beat shall have its step. This inaccuracy in the measure has exposed the *Valse à Deux Temps* to the just censure of musicians, but has never interfered with its success among dancers. We must caution our readers, however, against one mistake often made by the inexperienced. They imagine that it is unnecessary to observe any rule of time in this dance, and are perfectly careless whether they begin the step at the beginning, end, or middle of the bar. This is quite inadmissible. Every bar must contain within its three beats two steps. These steps must begin and end strictly with the beginning and end of each bar; otherwise a hopeless confusion of the measure will ensue. Precision in this matter is the more requisite, because of the peculiarity in the measure. If the first step in each bar be not strongly marked, the valse measure has no chance of making itself apparent; and the dance becomes a meaningless *galop*.

The step contains two movements, a *glissade* and a *chassez*, following each other quickly in the same direction. Gentleman begins as usual with his left foot; lady with her right.

1st beat.—*Glissade* to the left with left foot.

2d and 3d beats.—*Chassez* in the same direction with right foot; do not turn in this first bar.

2d bar, 1st beat.—Slide right foot backwards, turning half round.

2d and 3d beats.—Pass left foot behind right, and *chassez* forward with it, turning half round to complete the *figure en tournant*. Finish with right foot in front, and begin over again with left foot.

There is no variation in this step; but you can vary the movement by going backward or forward at pleasure, instead of continuing the rotary motion. The *Valse à Deux Temps*, like the Polka, admits of a reverse step; but it looks awkward unless executed to perfection. The first requisite in this Valse is to avoid all jumping movements. The feet must glide smoothly and swiftly over the floor, and be raised from it as little as possible. Being so very quick a dance, it must be performed quietly, otherwise it is liable to become ungraceful and vulgar. The steps should be short, and the knees slightly bent.

As the movement is necessarily very rapid, the danger of collision is proportionately increased; and gentlemen will do well to remember and act upon this hint.

They should also be scrupulous not to attempt to conduct a lady through this valse until they have thoroughly mastered the step and well practiced the *figure en tournant*. Awkwardness or inexperience doubles the risks of a collision; which, in this extremely rapid dance, might be attended with serious consequences.

The *Deux Temps* is a somewhat fatiguing valse, and after two or three turns around the room, the gentleman should pause to allow his partner to rest. He should be careful to select a lady whose height does not present too striking a contrast to his own; for it looks ridiculous to see a tall man dancing with a short woman, or *vice versâ*. This observation applies to all round dances, but especially to the valse, in any of its forms.

XVII. THE FINE STEP VALSE.

The step is extremely simple.

XVIII.—THE GALOP.

The Galop, as its name implies, is the quintessence of all the "fast" dances. At the time of the Polka mania it was very much in vogue, and almost as great a favorite as the *Deux Temps*. Although its popularity has greatly declined of late, it generally occurs twice or thrice in the programme of every ball-room; and the music of the Galop is, like the dance itself, so gay and spirited, that we should regret to see it wholly laid aside. The step is similar to that of the *Deux Temps* Valse, but the time is 2/4, and as quick as possible. Two *chassez* steps are made in each bar. The figure can be varied by taking four or eight steps in the same direction, or by turning with every two steps, as in the *Deux Temps*. Like all round dances, it admits of an unlimited number of couples. Being, perhaps, the most easy of any, every one takes part in it, and the room is generally crowded during its continuance. A special amount of care is therefore necessary on the part of the gentleman to protect his partner from accidents.

XIX.—THE COTILLON.

The Cotillon is never commenced till toward the close of the ball, at so advanced an hour that all the sober portion of the assembly have retired, and only the real lovers of dancing remain, who sometimes prolong this their favorite amusement till a late hour in the morning.

It is customary for gentlemen to select their partners for the Cotillon early in the evening, while the other dances are in progress; for, as it lasts so long a time, it is necessary to know beforehand how many ladies feel inclined to remain during its continuance.

A circle of chairs is arranged round the room, the center being left clear; the spectators stand behind the chairs, so as not to interfere with the dancers. Each gentleman leads his partner to a seat, taking another beside her. To these same seats they return after every figure, it being the etiquette of the dance that no couple should appropriate any chairs but their own, taken at the commencement. When the dancers are arranged round the room, the orchestra strikes up the spirited music of the Cotillon, which consists of a long series of valse movements at the usual *tempo* of the *Deux Temps*. There are generally several leaders of the Cotillon, who decide upon the succession of the figures. If there are many couples dancing, one leader attends upon a group of six or eight couples, to insure that all shall take part. We are aware of no fixed rule for the succession of the figures, which depends upon the caprice of the leaders. A good leader will invent new combinations, or diversify old figures; thus securing an almost endless variety. One of the most popular is the following:—

Several gentlemen assume the names of flowers or plants, such as the honeysuckle, woodbine, ivy, etc. A lady is then requested to name her favorite flower, and the fortunate swain who bears its name springs forward and valses off with her in triumph. It is usual to make one, or at most two, turns round the room, and then restore the lady to her own partner, who in the meantime has perhaps been the chosen one of another lady. All having regained their places, each gentleman valses with his own partner once round the room, or remains sitting by her side, as she may feel inclined.

Baskets filled with small bouquets are brought in. Each gentleman provides himself with a bouquet, and presents it to the lady with whom he wishes to valse.

Sometimes a light pole or staff is introduced, to the top of which are attached long streamers of different colored ribbons. A lady takes one of these to several of her fair companions in turn, each of whom chooses a ribbon, and, holding it firmly in her hand, follows the leading lady to the center of the room. Here they are met by an equal number of gentlemen, likewise grouped round a leader who carries the pole, while each holds a streamer of his favorite color, or that which he imagines would be selected by the *dame de ses pensées*. The merry groups compare notes: those who possess streamers of the same color pair off in couples, and valse gaily round the room, returning to places as before.

Six or eight ladies, and the same number of gentlemen, form in two lines, facing each other. The leading lady throws a soft worsted ball of bright colors at the gentleman with whom she wishes to dance. He catches it, throws it back to the fair group, and valses off with his partner. Whoever catches the returning ball has the right to throw next; and the same ceremony is repeated until all have chosen their partners, with whom they valse round the room, returning to places as usual. Sometimes a handkerchief is substituted for the ball; but the latter is better, being more easily thrown and caught.

Six or eight chairs are placed in a circle, the backs turned inwards. Ladies seat themselves in the chairs, gentlemen move slowly round in front of them. Each lady throws her handkerchief or bouquet at the gentleman with whom she wishes to dance as he passes before her; Valse round as usual, and return to places. Sometimes a gentleman is blindfolded and placed in a chair. Two ladies take a seat on either side of him, and he is bound to make his selection without seeing the face of his partner. Having done so, he pulls the covering from his eyes and valses off with her. It is a curious circumstance that mistakes seldom occur, the gentleman being generally sufficiently *clairvoyant* to secure the partner he desires.

We have here described a few of the most striking figures of the Cotillon. We might multiply them to an extent which would equally tax the patience of our readers and our own powers of remembrance, but we forbear. Gifts and souvenirs are usually freely distributed.

XX.—THE SPANISH DANCE.

This pretty, though now somewhat old-fashioned, dance was, before the introduction of the *Deux Temps* and polka, a principle feature in every ball-room. It is danced with the step and music of the old *Valse à Trois Temps*, played slower than the music of the *Deux Temps*.

Sometimes the couples stand in two long parallel lines, as in a country dance; sometimes they are arranged in a circle. The leading gentleman must be on the ladies' side, and his partner on the gentlemen's side. Every fourth lady and gentleman change places, to avoid the necessity of keeping the other couples waiting. The whole set can thus begin at the same moment.

Leading gentleman and *second* lady advance and retreat with valse step and change places. Leading lady and second gentleman do the same at the same time. Leading gentleman and his partner advance and retreat, and change places. Second lady and gentleman do the same at the same time. Leading gentleman and second lady repeat this figure, first lady and second gentleman likewise, at same time.

Leading gentleman and first lady repeat same figure; second gentleman and lady repeat at same time.

All four, joining hands, advance to center and retreat. Ladies pass to the left. Repeat three times. Each gentleman takes his partner, and the two couples valse round each other once or twice at pleasure, the second lady and gentleman being left at the top of the figure, as in a country dance. Leading gentleman and partner repeat same figure with succeeding couple to end of dance.

It is obvious that there must be an equal number of couples, and that they must be arranged in sets of four, eight, sixteen, twenty, twenty-four, and so on.

XXI.—LA TEMPÊTE.

La Tempête is divided into parties of four couples, like the quadrille, but their arrangement is different. Two couples stand side by side, facing their respective *vis-à-vis;* there are not any side couples. As many sets of four couples can be thus arranged as the room will accommodate. Each new set turns its back upon the second line of the preceding set. Thus the dance can be the whole length of the room, but it is only the breadth of two couples. The figure is as follows:—

Place two couples side by side, the lady standing at the right hand of the gentleman. Place two other couples as their *vis-à-vis*. Next place two couples with their backs turned to the first set; two couples opposite them for their *vis-à-vis*, and continue arranging more sets of four couples, according to the number of the dancers and the size of the room.

First part.—All the couples begin at the same moment, by advancing and retreating twice, with joined hands. First couples (that is all whose backs are turned to the top of the room), cross with hands joined to the places of their *vis-à-vis*. The latter cross at the same time, but, separating, pass outside two couples at the top, where they join hands, return to own places, and back again to the top without separating, the top couples crossing separately at the same time outside the second couples. Top couples then join hands, and all return to their own places, second couples separating to allow the others to pass between them.

Ladies and gentlemen in the center of each line join hands, giving their disengaged hands to their two *vis-à-vis*. All four half round to the left, then half-round back again to places. Meantime the outside lady and gentleman perform the same with their respective *vis-à-vis*, making a circle of two instead of four. Circle of four give hands across round; change hands; round once more, and back to places. Outside couples perform same figure in twos. All the sets perform the figure at the same moment.

Second part.—All advance, retreat, and advance again, all the top couples passing the second couples into the next line, where they recommence the same figure, their former *vis-à-vis* having passed to the top, and turned round to wait for a fresh *vis-à-vis*, gentleman always keeping lady at his right hand. An entire change of places is thus effected, which is continued throughout this figure, until all the top lines have passed to the bottom, the bottom lines at the same time passing to the top, and then turning round, all go back again by the same method reversed, till all have regained their original places. The dance may terminate here, or the last figure may be repeated at pleasure. When the first exchange of *vis-à-vis* takes place the new lines at the top and bottom find themselves for a moment without a *vis-à-vis;* but at the next move forward they are provided, and can continue the figure as above described. We extract from a contemporary the following graceful variation in the first half of this dance:—" All advance and retire twice (hands joined). All *vis-à-vis* couples *chassez croisez en double*, each gentleman retaining his partner's left hand; eight *galop* steps (four bars); *déchassez* eight steps (four bars); the couple on the right of the top line passing in front of the couple on the left the first time; returning to place, passing behind. Thus, two couples are moving to the right and two to the left. This is repeated. The *vis-à-vis* couples do likewise at the same time. This, of course, applies to all the couples, as all commence at the same time."

La Tempête is danced to quick music in 2/4 time. The step is the same as in quadrilles, varied sometimes by the introduction of the *galop* step, when the couples cross into each others' places or advance into the lines of the next set.

XXII.—SIR ROGER DE COVERLEY AND A VIRGINNY REEL.

Sir Roger de Coverley or the Virginny Reel is always introduced at the end of the evening, and no dance could be so well fitted to send the guests home in good humor with each other and with their hosts. We describe it as it is danced in the present day, slightly modernized to suit the taste of our time. Like the quadrille, it can be danced with equal propriety by old or young, and is so easy that the most inexperienced dancer may fearlessly venture to take part in it.

Form in two parallel lines; ladies on the left, gentlemen on the right, facing their partners. All advance; retreat (which occupies the first four bars); cross to opposite places (four bars more); advance and retreat (four bars); re-cross to places (four bars).

The lady who stands at the top and the gentleman who stands at the bottom, of each line, advance towards each other, courtesy and bow, and retire to places. The gentleman at the top and the lady at the bottom do the same. Lady at top and gentleman at bottom advance again, give right hands, and swing quickly round each other back to places. Gentleman at top and lady at bottom do the same. Top lady advances, gives right hand to partner opposite, and passes behind the two gentlemen standing next to him. Then through the line and across it, giving left hand to partner, who meets her half way between the two lines, having in the meantime passed behind the two ladies who stood next his partner. Lady then passes behind the two ladies next lowest; gentleman at same time behind the two gentlemen next lowest; and so on all down the line. At the bottom, lady gives left hand to her partner, and they promenade back to places at the top of the line. (This figure is frequently ommitted.) Top couple advance, courtesy and bow, then lady turns off to the right, gentleman to the left, each followed by the rest of her or his line. Top couple meet at the bottom of figure, join hands, and raising their arms, let all the other couples pass under them towards the top of the line, till all reach their own places, except the top, who have now become the bottom couple. Figure is repeated from the beginning, until the top couple have once more worked their way back to their original places at the top of the line.

GLOSSARY.

We subjoin a Glossary of all the French words and expressions that have long since been universally accepted as the accredited phraseology of the Ball-room.

A vos places, *back to your own places.*
A la fin, *at the end.*
A droite, *to the right.*
A gauche, *to the left.*
Balancez, *set to your partners.*
Balancez aux coins, *set to the corners.*
Balancez quatre en ligne, *four dancers set in a line, joining hands, as in La Poule.*
Balancez en moulinet, *gentlemen and their partners give each other right hands across, and* balancez *in the form of a cross.*
Balancez et tour des mains, *all set to partners, and turn to places.* (See Tour des mains.)
Ballotez, *do the same four times without changing your places.*
Chaine Anglaise, *opposite couples right and left.*
Chaine des dames, *ladies' chain.*
Chaine Anglaise double, *double right and left.*
Chaine des dames double, *all the ladies perform the ladies' chain at the same time.*
Chassez croisez, *do the* chassé *step from left to right, or right to left, the lady passing before the gentleman in the opposite direction, that is, moving right if he moves left, and vice versa.*
Chassez croisez et déchassez, *change places with partners, ladies passing in front, first to the right, then to the left, back to places. It may be either* à quatre—*four couples—or* les huit—*eight couples.*
Chassez à droite—à gauche, *move to the right—to the left.*
Le cavalier seul, *gentleman advances alone.*
Les cavaliers seuls deux fois, *gentlemen advance and retire twice without their partners.*
Changez vos dames, *change partners.*
Contre partie pour les autres, *the other dancers do the same figure.*
Demi promenade, *half promenade.*
Demi chaine Anglaise, *half right and left.*
Demi moulinet, *ladies all advance to center, right hands across, and back to places.*
Demi tour à quatre, *four hands half round.*
Dos-à-dos, *lady and opposite gentleman advance, pass round each other back to back, and return to places.*
Les dames en moulinet, *ladies give right hands across to each other, half round, and back again with left hands.*
Les dames donnent la main droit—gauche—à leurs cavalier, *ladies give the right—left—hands to partners.*
En avant deux et en arrière, *first lady and* vis-à-vis *gentleman advance and retire. To secure brevity,* en avant *is always understood to imply* en arrière *when the latter is not expressed.*
En avant deux fois, *advance and retreat twice.*
En avant quatre, *first couple and their* vis-à-vis *advance and retire.*
En avant trois, *three advance and retire, as in La Pastorale.*
Figurez devant, *dance before.*
Figurez à droite—à gauche, *dance to the right—to the left.*
La grande tour de rond, *all join hands and dance completely round the figure in a circle back to places.*
Le grand rond, *all join hands, and advance and retreat twice, as in La Finale.*
Le grand quatre, *all eight couples form into squares.*
La grande chaine, *all the couples move quite round the figure, giving alternately the right and left hand to each in succession, beginning with the right, until all have regained their places, as in last figure of the Lancers.*
La grande promenade, *all eight (or more) couples promenade all around the figure back to places.*
La main, *the hand.*
La meme pour les cavaliers, *gentlemen do the same.*
Le moulinet, *hand across. The figure will explain whether it is the gentlemen, or the ladies, or both, who are to perform it.*
Pas de Allemande, *the gentleman turns his partner under each arm in succession.*
Pas de Basque, *a kind of sliding step forward, terformed with both feet alternately in quick succession. Used in the Redowa and other dances. Comes from the South of France.*
Glissade, *a sliding step.*
Le Tiroir, *first couple cross with hands joined to opposite couple's place, opposite couple crossing separately outside them; then cross back to places, same figure reversed.*
Tour des mains, *give both hands to partner, and turn her round without quitting your places.*
Tour sur place, *the same.*
Tournez vos dames, *the same.*
Tour aux coins, *turn at the corners, as in the Caledonians, each gentleman turning the lady who stands nearest his left hand, and immediately returning to his own place.*
Traversez, *cross over to opposite place.*
Retraversez, *cross back again.*
Traversez deux, en donnant la main droite, *lady and* vis-à-vis *gentleman cross, giving right hand, as in La Poule.*
Vis-à-vis, *opposite.*
Figure en tournant, *circular form.*

MARRIAGE ETIQUETTE

LOVE IN A NOSEGAY.

PHOTO ELECTROTYPE ENG. CO. N.Y.

Etiquette of Courtship and Matrimony.

FIRST STEPS IN COURTSHIP.

IT would be out of place in these pages to grapple with a subject so large as that of Love in its various phases: a theme that must be left to poets, novelists, and moralists to dilate upon. It is sufficient for our purpose to recognize the existence of this, the most universal—the most powerful—of human passions, when venturing to offer our counsel and guidance to those of both sexes who, under its promptings, have resolved to become votaries of Hymen, but who, from imperfect knowledge of conventional usages, are naturally apprehensive that at every step they take they may render themselves liable to misconception, ridicule, or censure.

We will take it for granted, then, that a gentleman has in one way or another become fascinated by a fair lady—possibly a recent acquaintance—whom he is most anxious to know more particularly. His heart already feels "the inly touch of love," and his most ardent wish is to have that love returned.

At this point we venture to give him a word of serious advice. We urge him, before he ventures to take any step towards the pursuit of this object, to consider well his position and prospects in life, and reflect whether they are such as to justify him in deliberately seeking to win the young lady's affections, with the view of making her his wife at no distant period. Should he, after such a review of his affairs, feel satisfied that he can proceed honorably, he may then use fair opportunities to ascertain the estimation in which the young lady, as well as her family, is held by friends. It is perhaps needless to add, that all possible delicacy and caution must be observed in making such inquiries, so as to avoid compromising the lady herself in the slightest degree. When he has satisfied himself on this head, and found no insurmountable impediment in his way, his next endeavor will be, through the mediation of a common friend, to procure an introduction to the lady's family. Those who undertake such an office incur no slight responsibility, and are, of course, expected to be scrupulously careful in performing it, and to communicate all they happen to know affecting the character and circumstances of the individual they introduce.

We will now reverse the picture, and see how matters stand on the fair one's side.

First, let us hope that the inclination is mutual; at all events that the lady views her admirer with preference, that she deems him not unworthy of her favorable regard, and that his attentions are agreeable to her. It is true her heart may not yet be won: she has to be wooed; and what fair daughter of Eve has not hailed with rapture that brightest day in the springtide of her life? She has probably first met the gentleman at a ball, or other festive occasion, where the excitement of the scene has reflected on every object around a roseate tint. We are to suppose, of course, that in looks, manners, and address, her incipient admirer is not below her ideal standard in gentlemanly attributes. His respectful approaches to her—in soliciting her hand as a partner in the dance, etc.—have first awakened on her part a slight feeling of interest towards him. This mutual feeling of interest, once established, soon "grows by what it feeds on." The exaltation of the whole scene favors its development, and it can hardly be wondered at if both parties leave judgment "out in the cold." while enjoying each other's society, and possibly already pleasantly occupied in building "castles in the air." Whatever may eventually come of it, the fair one is conscious for the nonce of being unusually happy. This emotion is not likely to be diminished when she finds herself the object of general attention—accompanied, it may be, by the display of a little envy among rival beauties—owing to the assiduous homage of her admirer. At length, prudence whispers that he is to her, as yet, a comparative stranger; and with a modest reserve she endeavors to retire from his observation, so as not to seem to encourage his attentions. The gentleman's ardor, however, is not to be thus checked; he again solicits her to be his partner in a dance. She finds it hard, very hard, to refuse him; and both, yielding at last to the alluring influences by which they are surrounded, discover at the moment of parting that a new and delightful sensation has been awakened in their hearts.

At a juncture so critical in the life of a young, inexperienced woman as that when she begins to form an attachment for one of the opposite sex—at a moment when she needs the very best advice, accompanied with a considerate regard for her overwrought feelings—the very best course she can take is to confide the secret of her heart to that truest and most loving of friends—her mother. Fortunate is the daughter who has not been deprived of that wisest and tenderest of counselors—whose experience of life, whose prudence and sagacity, whose anxious care and appreciation of her child's sentiments, and whose awakened recollections of her own trysting days, qualify and entitle her, above all other beings, to counsel and comfort her trusting child, and to claim her confidence. Let the timid girl then pour forth into her mother's ear the flood of her pent-up feelings. Let her endeavor to distrust her own judgment, and seek hope, guidance, and support from one who, she well knows, will not deceive or mislead her. The confidence thus established will be productive of the most beneficial results—by securing the daughter's obedience to her parent's advice, and her willing adoption of the observances prescribed by etiquette, which, as the courtship progresses, that parent will not fail to recommend as strictly essential in this phase of life. Where a young woman has had the misfortune to be deprived of her mother, she should at such a period endeavor to find her next best counselor in some female relative, or other trustworthy friend.

We are to suppose that favorable opportunities for meeting have occurred, until, by and by, both the lady and her admirer have come to regard each other with such warm feelings of inclination as to have a constant craving for each other's society. Other eyes have in the meantime not failed to notice the symptoms of a growing attachment; and some "kind friends" have, no doubt, even set them down as already engaged.

The admirer of the fair one is, indeed, so much enamored as to be unable longer to retain his secret within his own breast; and not being without hope that his attachment is reciprocated, resolves on seeking an introduction to the lady's family preparatory to his making a formal declaration of love.

It is possible, however, that the lover's endeavors to procure the desired introduction may fail of success, although where no material difference of social position exists, this difficulty will be found to occur less frequently than might at first be supposed. He must then discreetly adopt measures to bring himself, in some degree, under the fair one's notice: such, for instance, as attending the place of worship which she frequents, meeting her, so often as to be manifestly for the purpose, in the course of her promenades, etc. He will thus soon be able to judge—even without speaking to the lady—whether his further attentions will be distasteful to her. The signs of this on the lady's part, though of the most trifling nature, and in no way compromising her, will be unmistakable: for, as the poet tells us in speaking of the sex:—

"He gave them but one tongue to say us 'Nay,'
And two fond eyes to grant!"

Should her demeanor be decidedly discouraging, any perseverance on his part would be ungentlemanly and highly indecorous. But, on the other hand, should a timid blush intimate doubt, or a gentle smile lurking in the half-dropped eye give pleasing challenge to further parley, when possible he may venture to write—not to the lady—that would be the opening of a clandestine correspondence; an unworthy course, where every act should be open and straightforward, as tending to manly and honorable ends—but to the father or guardian, through the agency of a common friend where feasible, or, in some instances, to the party at whose residence the lady may be staying. In his letter he ought first to state his position in life and prospects, as well as mention his family connections; and then request permission to visit the family, as a preliminary step to paying his addresses to the object of his admiration.

By this course he in no wise compromises either himself or the lady, but leaves open to both, at any future period, an opportunity of retiring from the position of courtship taken up on the one side, and of receiving addresses on the other, without laying either party open to the accusation of fickleness or jilting.

ETIQUETTE OF COURTSHIP.

In whatever way the attachment may have originated, whether resulting from old association or from a recent acquaintanceship between the lovers, we will assume that the courtship is so far in a favorable train that the lady's admirer has succeeded in obtaining an introduction to her family, and that he is about to be received in their domestic circle on the footing of a welcome visitor, if not yet in the light of a probationary suitor.

In the first place, matters will in all probability be found to amble on so calmly, that the enamored pair may seldom find it needful to consult the rules of etiquette; but in the latter, its rules must be attentively observed, or "the course of true love" will assuredly not run smooth.

Young people are naturally prone to seek the company of those they love; and as their impulses are often at such times impatient of control, etiquette prescribes cautionary rules for the purpose of averting the mischief that unchecked intercourse and incautious familiarity might give rise to. For instance, a couple known to be attached to each other should never, unless when old acquaintances, be left alone for any length of time, nor be allowed to meet in any other place than the lady's home—particularly at balls, concerts, and other public places—except in the presence of a third party. This, as a general rule, should be carefully observed, although exceptions may occasionally occur under special circumstances.

WHAT THE LADY SHOULD OBSERVE DURING COURTSHIP.

A lady should be particular during the early days of courtship—while still retaining some clearness of mental vision—to observe the manner in which her suitor comports himself to other ladies. If he behave with ease and courtesy, without freedom or the slightest approach to license in manner or conversation; if he never speak slightingly of the sex, and is ever ready to honor its virtues and defend its weakness ; she may continue to incline towards him a willing ear. His habits and his conduct must awaken her vigilant attention before it be too late. Should he come to visit her at irregular hours ; should he exhibit a vague or wandering attention—give proofs of a want of punctuality—show disrespect for age—sneer at things sacred, or absent himself from regular attendance at divine service—or evince an inclination to expensive pleasures beyond his means, or to low and vulgar amusements ; should he be foppish, eccentric, or very slovenly in his dress ; or display a frivolity of mind, and an absence of well-directed energy in his worldly pursuits ; let the young lady, we say, while there is yet time, eschew that gentleman's acquaintance, and allow it gently to drop. The effort, at whatever cost to her feelings, must be made, if she have any regard for her future happiness and self-respect. The proper course then to take is to intimate her distate, and the causes that have given rise to it, to her parents or guardian, who will be pretty sure to sympathize with her, and to take measures for facilitating the retirement of the gentleman from his pretensions.

WHAT THE GENTLEMAN SHOULD OBSERVE DURING COURTSHIP.

It would be well also for the suitor, on his part, during the first few weeks of courtship, carefully to observe the conduct of the young lady in her own family, and the degree of estimation in which she is held by them, as well as among her intimate friends. If she be attentive to her duties ; respectful and affectionate to her parents ; kind and forbearing to her brothers and sisters ; not easily ruffled in temper ; if her mind be prone to cheerfulness and to hopeful aspiration, instead of to the display of a morbid anxiety and dread of coming evil ; if her pleasures and enjoyments be those which chiefly center in home ; if her words be characterized by benevolence, good-will, and charity : then we say, let him not hesitate, but hasten to enshrine so precious a gem in the casket of his affections. But if, on the other hand, he should find that he has been attracted by the tricksome affectation and heartless allurements of a flirt, ready to bestow smiles on all, but with a heart for none ; if she who has succeeded for a time in fascinating him be of uneven temper, easily provoked, and slow to be appeased ; fond of showy dress, and eager for admiration ; ecstatic about trifles, frivolous in her tastes, and weak and wavering in performing her duties ; if her religious observances are merely the formality of lip-service ; if she be petulant to her friends, pert and disrespectful to her parents, overbearing to her inferiors ; if pride, vanity, and affectation be her characteristics ; if she be inconstant in her friendships ; gaudy and slovenly, rather than neat and scrupulously clean, in attire and personal habits ; then we counsel the gentleman to retire as speedily, but as politely, as possible from the pursuit of an object unworthy of his admiration and love ; nor dread that the lady's friends—who must know her better than he can do—will call him to account for withdrawing from the field.

But we will take it for granted that all goes on well ; that the parties are, on sufficient acquaintance, pleased with each other, and that the gentleman is eager to prove the sincerity of his affectionate regard by giving some substantial token of his love and homage to the fair one. This brings us to the question of

PRESENTS,

a point on which certain observances of etiquette must not be disregarded. A lady, for instance, cannot with propriety accept presents from a gentleman *previously* to his having made proposals of marriage. She would by so doing incur an obligation at once embarrassing and unbecoming. Should, however, the gentleman insist on making her a present—as of some trifling object of jewelry, etc.—there must be no secret about it. Let the young lady take an early opportunity of saying to her admirer, in the presence of her father or mother, "I am much obliged to you for that ring (or other trinket, as the case may be) which you kindly offered me the other day, and which I shall be most happy to accept, if my parents do not object ; " and let her say this in a manner which, while it increases the obligation, will divest it altogether of impropriety, from having been conferred under the sanction of her parents.

We have now reached that stage in the progress of the Courtship, where budding affection, having developed into mature growth, encourages the lover to make

THE PROPOSAL.

When about to take this step, the suitor's first difficulty is how to get a favorable opportunity ; and next, having got the chance, how to screw his courage up to give utterance to the "declaration." A declaration in writing should certainly be avoided where the lover can by any possibility get at the lady's ear. But there are cases where this is so difficult that an impatient lover cannot be restrained from adopting the agency of a *billet-doux* in declaring his passion.

The lady, before proposal, is generally prepared for it. It is seldom that such an avowal comes without some previous indications of look and manner on the part of the admirer, which can hardly fail of being understood. She may not, indeed, consider herself engaged; and although nearly certain of the conquest she has made, may yet have her misgivings. Some gentlemen dread to ask, lest they should be refused. Many pause just at the point, and refrain from anything like ardor in their professions of attachment until they feel confident, that they may be spared the mortification and ridicule that is supposed to attach to being rejected, in addition to the pain of disappointed hope. This hesitation when the mind is made up is wrong ; but it does often occur, and we suppose ever will do so, with persons of great timidity of character. By it both parties are kept needlessly on the fret, until the long-looked-for opportunity unexpectedly arrives, when the flood-gates of feeling are loosened, and the full tide of mutual affection gushes forth uncontrolled. It is, however, at this moment—the agony-point to the embarrassed lover, who "doats yet doubts"—whose suppressed feelings rendered him morbidly sensitive—that a lady should be especially careful lest any show of either prudery or coquetry on her part should lose to her forever the object of her choice. True love is generally delicate and timid, and may easily be scared by affected indifference, through feelings of wounded pride. A lover needs very little to assure him of the reciprocation of his attachment : a glance, a single pressure of the hand, a whispered syllable, on the part of the loved one, will suffice to confirm his hopes,

REFUSAL BY THE YOUNG LADY.

When a lady rejects the proposal of a gentleman, her behavior should be characterized by the most delicate feeling toward sone who, in offering her his hand, has proved his desire to confer upon her, by this implied preference for her above all other women, the greatest honor it is in his power to offer. Therefore, if she have no love for him, she ought at least to evince a tender regard for his feelings ; and in the event of her being previously engaged, should at once acquaint him with the fact. No right-minded man would desire to persist in a suit, when he well knew that the object of his admiration had already disposed of her heart.

When a gentleman makes an offer of his hand by letter, the letter must be answered, and certainly not returned, should the answer be a refusal ; unless, indeed, when from a previous repulse, or some other particular and special circumstance, such an offer may be regarded by the lady or her relatives as presumptuous and intrusive. Under such circumstances, the letter may be placed by the lady in the hands of her parents or guardian, to be dealt with by them as they may deem most advisable.

No woman of proper feeling would regard her rejection of an offer of marriage from a worthy man as a matter of triumph ; her feeling on such an occasion should be one of regretful sympathy with him for the pain she is unavoidably compelled to inflict. Nor should such a rejection be unaccompanied with some degree of self-examination on her part, to discern whether any lightness of demeanor or tendency to flirtation may have given rise to a false hope of her favoring his suit. At all events, no lady should ever treat the man who has so honored her with the slightest disrespect or frivolous disregard, nor ever unfeelingly parade a more favored suitor before one whom she has refused.

CONDUCT OF THE GENTLEMAN WHEN HIS ADDRESSES ARE REJECTED.

The conduct of the gentleman under such distressing circumstances should be characterized by extreme delicacy and a chivalrous resolve to avoid occasioning any possible annoyance or uneasiness to the fair author of his pain. If, however, he should have reason to suppose that his rejection has resulted from mere indifference to his suit, he need not altogether retire from the field, but may endeavor to kindle a feeling of regard and sympathy for the patient endurance of his disappointment, and for his continued but respectful endeavors to please the lukewarm fair one. But in case of avowed or evident preference for another, it becomes imperative upon him, as a gentleman, to withdraw at once, and so relieve the lady of any obstacle, that his presence or pretensions may occasion, to the furtherance of her obvious wishes. A pertinacious continuance of his attentions, on the part of one who has been distinctly rejected, is an insult deserving of the severest reprobation. Although the weakness of her sex, which ought to be her protection, frequently prevents a woman from forcibly breaking off an acquaintance thus annoyingly forced upon her, she rarely fails to resent such impertinence by that sharpest of woman's weapons, a keen-edged but courteous ridicule, which few men can bear up against.

REFUSAL BY THE LADY'S PARENTS OR GUARDIANS.

It may happen that both the lady and her suitor are willing, but that the parents or guardians of the former, on being referred to, deem the connection unfitting, and refuse their consent. In this state of matters, the first thing a man of sense, proper feeling, and candor should do, is to endeavor to learn the objections of the parents, to see whether they cannot be removed. If they are based on his present insufficiency of means, a lover of a persevering spirit may effect much in removing apprehension on that score, by cheerfully submitting to a reasonable time of probation, in the hope of amelioration in his worldly circumstances. Happiness delayed will be none the less precious when love has stood the test of constancy and the trial of time. Should the objection be founded on inequality of social position, the parties, if young, may wait until matured age shall ripen their judgment and place the future more at their own disposal. A clandestine marriage should be peremptorily declined. In too many cases it is a fraud committed by an elder and more experienced party upon one whose ignorance of the world's ways, and whose confiding tenderness appeal to him for protection even against himself. In nearly all the instances we have known of such marriages, the result proved the step to have been ill-judged, imprudent, and highly injurious to the reputation of one party, and in the long run detrimental to the happiness of both.

CONDUCT OF THE ENGAGED COUPLE.

The conduct of the bridegroom-elect should be marked by a gallant and affectionate assiduity towards his lady-love—a *denouement* easily felt and understood, but not so easy to define. That of the lady towards him should manifest delicacy, tenderness, and confidence : while looking for his thorough devotion to herself, she should not captiously take offense and show airs at his showing the same kind of attention to other ladies as she, in her turn, would not hesitate to receive from the other sex.

In the behavior of a gentleman towards his betrothed in public, little difference should be perceptible from his demeanor to other ladies, except in those minute attentions which none but those who love can properly understand or appreciate.

In private, the slightest approach to indecorous familiarity must be avoided ; indeed it is pretty certain to be resented by every woman who deserves to be a bride. The lady's honor is now in her lover's hands, and he should never forget in his demeanor to and before her that that lady is to be his future wife.

It is the privilege of the betrothed lover, as it is also his duty, to give advice to the fair one who now implicitly confides in him. Should he detect a fault, should he observe failings which he would wish removed or amended, let him avail himself of this season, so favorable for the frank interchange of thought between the betrothed pair, to urge their correction. He will find a ready listener; and any judicious counsel offered to her by him will now be gratefully received, and remembered in after life. After marriage it may be too late; for advice on trivial points of conduct may then not improbably be resented by the wife as an unnecessary interference; now, the fair and loving creature is disposed like pliant wax in his hands to mold herself to his reasonable wishes in all things.

CONDUCT OF THE LADY DURING HER BETROTHAL.

A lady is not expected to keep aloof from society on her engagement, nor to debar herself from the customary attentions and courtesies of her male acquaintances generally; but she should, while accepting them cheerfully, maintain such a prudent reserve, as to intimate that they are viewed by her as mere acts of ordinary courtesy and friendship. In all places of public amusement—at balls, the opera, etc.—for a lady to be seen with any other cavalier than her avowed lover, in close attendance upon her, would expose her to the imputation of flirtation. She will naturally take pains at such a period to observe the taste of her lover in regard to her costume, and strive carefully to follow it, for all men desire to have their taste and wishes on such apparent trifles gratified. She should at the same time observe much delicacy in regard to dress, and be careful to avoid any unseemly display of her charms; lovers are naturally jealous of observation under such circumstances. It is a mistake not seldom made by women, to suppose their suitors will be pleased by the glowing admiration expressed by other men for the object of *their* passion. Most lovers, on the contrary, we believe, would prefer to withdraw their prize from general observation until the happy moment for their union has arrived.

CONDUCT OF THE GENTLEMAN TOWARDS THE FAMILY OF HIS BETROTHED.

The lover, having now secured his position, should use discretion and tact in his intercourse with the lady's family, and take care that his visits be not deemed too frequent—so as to be really inconvenient to them. He should accommodate himself as much as possible to their habits and ways, and be ever ready and attentive to consult their wishes. Marked attention, and in most cases affectionate kindness, to the lady's mother ought to be shown; such respectful homage will secure for him many advantages in his present position. He must not, however, presume to take his stand yet as a member of the family, nor exhibit an obtrusive familiarity in manner and conversation. Should a disruption of the engagement from some unexpected cause ensue, it is obvious that any such premature assumption would lead to very embarrassing results. In short, his conduct should be such as to win for himself the esteem and affection of all the family, and dispose them ever to welcome and desire his presence, rather than regard him as an intruder.

CONDUCT OF THE LADY ON RETIRING FROM HER ENGAGEMENT.

Should this step unhappily be found necessary on the lady's part, the truth should be spoken, and the reasons frankly given; there must be no room left for the suspicion of its having originated in caprice or injustice. The case should be so put that the gentleman himself must see and acknowledge the justice of the painful decision arrived at. Incompatible habits, ungentlemanly actions, anything tending to diminish that respect for the lover which should be felt for the husband; inconstancy, ill-governed temper—all of which, not to mention other obvious objections—are to be considered as sufficient reasons for terminating an engagement. The communication should be made as tenderly as possible; room may be left in mere venial cases for reformation; but all that is done must be so managed that not the slightest shadow of fickleness or want of faith may rest upon the character of the lady. It must be remembered, however, that the termination of an engagement by a lady has the privilege of passing unchallenged; a lady not being *bound* to declare any other reason than her will. Nevertheless she owes it to her own reputation that her decision should rest on a sufficient foundation, and be unmistakeably pronounced.

CONDUCT OF THE GENTLEMAN ON RETIRING FROM HIS ENGAGEMENT.

We hardly know how to approach this portion of our subject. The reasons must be strong indeed that can sufficiently justify a man, placed in the position of an accepted suitor, in severing the ties by which he has bound himself to a lady with the avowed intention of making her his wife. His reasons for breaking off his engagement must be such as will not merely satisfy his own conscience, but will justify him in the eyes of the world. If the fault be on the lady's side, great reserve and delicacy will be observed by any man of honor. If, on the other hand, the imperative force of circumstances, such as loss of fortune, or some other unexpected calamity to himself, may be the cause, then must the reason be clearly and fully explained, in such a manner as to soothe the painful feelings which such a result must necessarily occasion to the lady and her friends. It is scarcely necessary to point out the necessity for observing great caution in all that relates to the antecedents of an engagement that has been broken off; especially the return on either side of presents and of all letters that have passed.

This last allusion brings us to the consideration of

CORRESPONDENCE.

Letter-writing is one great test of ability and cultivation, as respects both sexes. The imperfections of education may be to some extent concealed or glossed over in conversation, but cannot fail to stand out conspicuously in a letter. An ill-written letter infallibly betrays the vulgarity and ignorance indicative of a mean social position.

But there is something more to be guarded against than even bad writing and worse spelling in a correspondence: *saying too much*—writing that kind of matter which will not bear to be read by other eyes than those for which it was originally intended. That this is too frequently done is amply proved by the love letters often read in a court of law, the most affecting passages from which occasion "roars of laughter" and the derisive comments of merry-making counsel. Occurrences of this kind prove how frequently letters are not returned or burned when an affair of the heart is broken off. Correspondence between lovers should at all events be tempered with discretion; and on the lady's part particularly, her affectionate expressions should not degenerate into a silly style of fondness.

It is as well to remark here, that in correspondence between a couple not actually engaged, the use of Christian names in addressing each other should be avoided.

DEMEANOR OF THE SUITOR DURING COURTSHIP.

The manners of a gentleman are ever characterized by urbanity and a becoming consideration for the feelings and wishes of others, and by a readiness to practice self-denial. But the very nature of courtship requires the fullest exercise of these excellent qualities on his part. The lover should carefully accommodate his tone and bearing, whether cheerful or serious, to the mood for the time of his lady-love, whose slightest wish must be his law. In his assiduities to her he must allow of no stint; though hindered by time, distance, or fatigue, he must strive to make his professional and social duties bend to his homage at the shrine of love. All this can be done, moreover, by a man of excellent sense with perfect propriety. Indeed, the world will not only commend him for such devoted gallantry, but will be pretty sure to censure him for any short-coming in his performance of such devoirs.

It is, perhaps, needless to observe that at such a period a gentleman should be scrupulously neat, without appearing particular, in his attire. We shall not attempt to prescribe what he should wear, as that must, of course, depend on the times of the day when his visits are paid, and other circumstances, such as meeting a party of friends, going to the theater, etc., with the lady.

SHOULD A COURTSHIP BE SHORT OR LONG?

The answer to this question must depend on the previous acquaintanceship, connection, or relationship of the parties, as well as on their present circumstances, and the position of their parents. In case of relationship or old acquaintanceship subsisting between the families, when the courtship, declaration, and engagement have followed each other rapidly, a short wooing is preferable to a long one, should other circumstances not create an obstacle. Indeed, as a general rule, we are disposed strongly to recommend a short courtship. A man is never well settled in the saddle of his fortunes until he be married. He wants spring, purpose, and aim; and, above all, he wants a *home* as the center of his efforts. Some portion of inconvenience, therefore, may be risked to obtain this; in fact, it often occurs that by waiting too long the freshness of life is worn off, and that the generous glow of early feelings becomes tamed down to lukewarmness by a too prudent delaying; while a slight sacrifice of ambition or self-indulgence on the part of the gentleman, and a little descent from pride of station on the lady's side, might have insured years of satisfied love and happy wedded life.

On the other hand, we would recommend a long courtship as advisable when—the friends on both sides favoring the match—it happens that the fortune of neither party will prudently allow an immediate marriage. The gentleman, we will suppose, has his way to make in his profession or business, and is desirous not to involve the object of his affection in the distressing inconvenience, if not the misery, of straitened means. He reflects that for a lady it is an actual degradation, however love may ennoble the motive of her submission, to descend from her former footing in society. He feels, therefore, that this risk ought not to be incurred. For, although the noble and loving spirit of a wife might enable her to bear up cheerfully against misfortune, and by her endearments soothe the broken spirit of her husband; yet the lover who would willfully, at the outset of wedded life, expose his devoted helpmate to the ordeal of poverty, would be deservedly scouted as selfish and unworthy. These, then, are among the circumstances which warrant a lengthened engagement, and it should be the endeavor of the lady's friends to approve such cautious delay, and do all they can to assist the lover in his efforts to abridge it. The lady's father should regard the lover in the light of another son added to his family, and spare no pains to promote his interests in life, while the lady's mother should do everything in her power, by those small attentions which a mother understands so well, to make the protracted engagement agreeable to him, and as endurable as possible to her daughter.

PRELIMINARY ETIQUETTE OF A WEDDING.

Whether the term of courtship may have been long or short —according to the requirements of the case—the time will at last arrive for

FIXING THE DAY.

While it is the gentleman's province to press for the earliest possible opportunity, it is the lady's privilege to name the happy day; not but that the bridegroom-elect must, after all, issue the fiat, for he has much to consider and prepare for beforehand: for instance, to settle where it will be most convenient to spend the honeymoon—a point which must depend on the season of the year, on his own vocation, and other circumstances. At this advanced state of affairs, we must not overlook the important question of

THE BRIDAL TROUSSEAU AND THE WEDDING PRESENTS.

Wedding presents must be sent always to the *bride*, never to the bridegroom, though they be given by friends of the latter. They should be sent during the week previous to the wedding day, as it is customary to display them before the ceremony.

Two cards folded in the invitation in the envelope are sent

with the wedding invitation. The invitation is in the name of the bride's mother, or, if she is not living, the relative or friend nearest the bride :

MRS. NICHOLAS RUTH

AT HOME,

Tuesday, November 18th,

FROM 11 TILL 2 O'CLOCK.

No. 86 W. 47TH STREET.

The two cards, one large and one small, are folded in this invitation. Upon the large card is engraved :

MR. AND MRS. W. F. JOHNSON

On the smaller one :

MISS ROSIE RUTH.

If the young people "receive" after their return from the bridal tour, and there is no wedding-day reception, the following card is sent out :

MR. AND MRS. W. F. JOHNSON

AT HOME,

Thursday, December 28th,

FROM 11 TILL 2 O'CLOCK,

No. 50 E. 63D STREET.

Or,

MR. AND MRS. W. F. JOHNSON

AT HOME,

Thursdays in December.

FROM 11 TILL 2 O'CLOCK.

No. 50 E. 63D STREET.

The bridal calls are not expected to be returned until the last day of reception.

The bridegroom gives to the first groomsman the control of the ceremony and money for the necessary expenses. The first groomsman presents the bouquet to the bride, leads the visitors up to the young couple for the words of congratulation, gives the clergyman his fee, engages the carriages, secures tickets, checks baggage, secures pleasant seats, if the happy pair start by rail for the "moon ;" and, in short, makes all arrangements.

If the wedding takes place in church, the front seats in the body of the church are reserved for the relatives of the young couple. The bride must not be kept waiting. The clergyman should be within the rails, the bridegroom and groomsmen should be in the vestry-room by the time the bride is due at the church. The bridesmaids should receive the bride in the vestibule.

The bridal party meet in the vestry-room. Then the bride, leaning on the arm of her father, leads the procession ; the bridegroom, with the bride's mother upon his arm, follows ; then groomsmen and bridesmaids in couples follow.

At the altar the bridegroom receives the bride, and the ceremony begins. The groomsmen stand behind the bridegroom, the bridesmaids behind the bride. In some churches, the bride and bridegroom remove the right hand glove ; in others it is not considered essential. The bride stands on the left of the groom.

When the wedding takes place at the house of the bride, the bridal party is grouped behind folding doors or curtains ere their friends see them. If, however, this is not convenient, they enter in the same order as in church.

The first bridesmaid removes the bride's left hand glove for the ring.

After the ceremony the bride and groom go in the same carriage from the church to the house, or from the house to the railway depot or boat.

The bride does not change her dress until she assumes her traveling dress. Her wedding gown is worn at the breakfast.

Friends of the family should call upon the mother of the bride during the two weeks after the wedding.

Mourning must not be worn at a wedding. Even in the case of a widowed mother to either of the happy pair, it is customary to wear gray, or some neutral tint.

It is no longer the fashion at a wedding or wedding reception to congratulate the bride ; it is the bridegroom who receives congratulations ; the bride wishes for her future happiness. The bride is spoken to first.

The day being fixed for the wedding, the bride's father now presents her with a sum of money for her trousseau, according to her rank in life. A few days previously to the wedding, presents are also made to the bride by relations and intimate friends, varying in amount and value according to their degrees of relationship and friendship—such as plate, furniture, jewelry, and articles of ornament, as well as of utility, to the newly-married lady in her future station. These, together with her wedding dresses, etc., it is customary to exhibit to the intimate friends of the bride a day or two before her marriage.

DUTY OF A BRIDEGROOM-ELECT.

The bridegroom-elect has, on the eve of matrimony, no little business to transact. His first care is to look after a house suitable for his future home, and then, assisted by the taste of his chosen helpmate, to take steps to furnish it in a becoming style. He must also, if engaged in business, make arrangements for a month's absence ; in fact, bring together all matters into a focus, so as to be readily manageable when, after the honeymoon, he shall take the reins himself. He will do well to burn most of his bachelor letters, and to part with, it may be, some few of his bachelor connections ; and he should communicate, in an easy, informal way, to his acquaintances generally, the close approach of so important a change in his condition. Not to do this might hereafter lead to inconvenience and cause no little annoyance.

We must now speak of

BUYING THE RING.

It is the gentleman's business to buy the ring; *and let him take special care not to forget it ;* for such an awkward mistake has frequently happened. The ring should be, we need scarcely say, of the very purest gold, but substantial. There are three reasons for this: first, that it may not break—a source of great trouble to the young wife; secondly, that it may not slip off the finger without being missed—few husbands being pleased to hear that their wives have lost their wedding rings; and thirdly, that it may last out the lifetime of the loving recipient, even should that life be protracted to the extreme extent. To get the right size required is not one of the least interesting of the delicate mysteries of love. A not unusual method is to get a sister of the fair one to lend one of the lady's rings to enable the jeweler to select the proper size. Care must be taken, however, that it is not too large. Some audacious suitors, rendered bold by their favored position, have been even known presumptuously to try the ring on the patient finger of the bride elect; and it has rarely happened in such cases that the ring has been refused, or sent back to be changed.

WHO SHOULD BE ASKED TO THE WEDDING.

The wedding should take place at the house of the bride's parents or guardians. The parties who ought to be asked are the father and mother of the gentleman, the brothers and sisters (their wives and husbands also, if married), and indeed the immediate relations and favored friends of both parties. Old family friends on the bride's side should also receive invitations—the *rationale* or original intention of this wedding assemblage being to give publicity to the fact that the bride is leaving her paternal home with the consent and approbation of her parents.

On this occasion the bridegroom has the privilege of asking any friends he may choose to the wedding; but no friend has a right to feel affronted at not being invited, since, were all the friends on either side assembled, the wedding breakfast would be an inconveniently crowded reception rather than an impressive ceremonial. It is, however, considered a matter of friendly attention on the part of those who cannot be invited, to be present at the ceremony in the church.

WHO SHOULD BE BRIDESMAIDS.

The bridesmaids should include the unmarried sisters of the bride; but it is considered an anomaly for an elder sister to perform this function. The pleasing novelty for several years past of an addition to the number of bridesmaids, varying from two to eight, and sometimes more, has added greatly to the interest in weddings, the bride being thus enabled to diffuse a portion of her own happiness among the most intimate of her younger friends. One lady is always appointed principal bridesmaid, and has the bride in her charge; it is also her duty to take care that the other bridesmaids have the wedding favors in readiness. On the second bridesmaid devolves, with her principal, the duty of sending out the cards; and on the third bridesmaid, in conjunction with the remaining beauties of her choir, the onerous office of attending to certain ministrations and mysteries connected with the wedding cake.

OF THE BRIDEGROOMSMEN.

It behooves a bridegroom to be exceedingly particular in the selection of the friends who, as groomsmen, are to be his companions and assistants on the occasion of his wedding. Their number is limited to that of the bridesmaids; one for each. It is unnecessary to add that very much of the social pleasure of the day will depend on their proper mating. Young and unmarried they must be, handsome they should be, good-humored they cannot fail to be, well dressed they will of course take good care to be. Let the bridegroom diligently con over his circle of friends, and select the comeliest and the pleasantest fellows for his own train. The principal bridegroomsman, styled his "best man," has, for the day, the special charge of the bridegroom; and the last warning we would give him is, to take care that, when the bridegroom puts on his wedding waistcoat, he does not omit to put the wedding ring into the corner of the left-hand pocket. The dress of a groomsman should be light and elegant; a dress coat, formerly considered indispensable, is no longer adopted.

ETIQUETTE OF A WEDDING.

The parties being assembled on the wedding morning in the drawing-room of the residence of the bride's father (unless, as sometimes happens, the breakfast is spread in that room), the happy *cortège* should proceed to the church in the following order:—

In the first carriage, the bride's mother and the parents of the bridegroom.

In the second and third carriages, bridesmaids.

Other carriages with the bride's friends.

In the last carriage, the bride and her father.

COSTUME OF THE BRIDE.

A bride's costume should be white, or some hue as close as possible to it.

COSTUME OF THE BRIDEGROOM.

Formerly it was not considered to be in good taste for a gentleman to be married in a black coat. More latitude is now allowed in the costume of a bridegroom, the style now adopted being what is termed morning dress: a frock coat, light trowsers, white waistcoat, ornamental tie, and white or gray gloves.

THE MARRIAGE CEREMONY.

The bridegroom stands at the right hand of the bride. The father stands just behind her, so as to be in readiness to give her hand at the proper moment to the bridegroom. The principal bridesmaid stands on the left of the bride, ready to take off the bride's glove, which she keeps as a perquisite and prize of her office.

THE WORDS "I WILL"

are to be pronounced distinctly and audibly by both parties, such being the all-important part of the ceremony as respects themselves: the public delivery, before the priest, by the father of his daughter to the bridegroom, being an evidence of his assent; the silence which follows the inquiry for "cause or just impediment" testifying that of society in general; and the "I will" being the declaration of the bride and bridegroom that they are voluntary parties to their holy union in marriage.

THE WORDS "HONOR AND OBEY"

must also be distinctly spoken by the bride. They constitute an essential part of the obligation and contract of matrimony on her part.

AFTER THE CEREMONY

the clergyman usually shakes hands with the bride and bridegroom, and the bride's father and mother, and a general congratulation ensues.

THE RETURN HOME.

The bridegroom now leads the bride out of the church, and the happy pair return homeward in the first carriage. The father and mother follow in the next. The rest "stand not on the order of their going," but start off in such wise as they can best contrive.

THE WEDDING BREAKFAST.

The bride and bridegroom sit together at the center of the table, in front of the wedding cake, the clergyman who performed the ceremony taking his place opposite to them. The top and bottom of the table are occupied by the father and mother of the bride. The principal bridesmaid sits to the left of the bride, and the principal bridegroomsman on the left of the bridegroom. It may not be unnecessary to say that it is customary for the ladies to wear their bonnets just as they came from the church. The bridesmaids cut the cake into small pieces, which are not eaten until the health of the bride is proposed. This is usually done by the officiating clergyman, or by an old and cherished friend of the family of the bridegroom. The bridegroom returns thanks for the bride and for himself. The health of the bride's parents is then proposed, and is followed by those of the principal personages present, the toast of the bridesmaids being generally one of the pleasantest features of the festal ceremony. After about two hours, the principal bridesmaid leads the bride out of the room as quietly as possible, so as not to disturb the party or attract attention. Shortly after—it may be in about ten minutes—the absence of the bride being noticed, the rest of the ladies retire. Then it is that the bridegroom has a few *melancholy* moments to bid adieu to his bachelor friends, and he then generally receives some hints on the subject in a short address from one of them, to which he is of course expected to respond. He then withdraws for a few moments, and returns after having made a slight addition to his toilet, in readiness for traveling.

DEPARTURE FOR THE HONEYMOON.

The young bride, divested of her bridal attire, and quietly costumed for the journey, now bids farewell to her bridesmaids and lady friends. A few tears spring to her gentle eyes as she takes a last look at the home she is now leaving. The servants venture to crowd about her with their humble but heartfelt congratulations; finally, she falls weeping on her mother's bosom. A short cough is heard, as of some one summoning up resolution to hide emotion. It is her father. He dares not trust his voice; but holds out his hand, gives her an affectionate kiss, and then leads her, half turning back, down the stairs and through the hall, to the door, where he delivers her as a precious charge to her husband, who hands her quickly into the carriage, springs in after her, waves his hand to the party who appear crowding at the window, half smiles at the throng about the door, then, amidst a shower of old slippers—missiles of good-luck sent flying after the happy pair—gives the word, and they are off, and started on the long-hoped-for voyage!

PRACTICAL ADVICE TO A NEWLY-MARRIED COUPLE.

Our advice to the husband will be brief. Let him have no concealments from his wife, but remember that their interests are mutual; that, as she must suffer the pains of every loss, as well as share the advantages of every success, in his career in life, she has therefore a right to know the risks she may be made to undergo. We do not say that it is necessary, or advisable, or even fair, to harass a wife's mind with the details of business; but where a change of circumstances—not for the better—is anticipated or risked, let her by all means be made acquainted with the fact in good time. Many a kind husband almost breaks his young wife's fond heart by an alteration in his manner, which she cannot but detect, but from ignorance of the cause very probably attributes to a wrong motive; while he, poor fellow, all the while out of pure tenderness, is endeavoring to conceal from her tidings—which must come out at last—of ruined hopes or failure in speculation; whereas, had she but known the danger beforehand, she would have alleviated his fears on her account, and by cheerful resignation have taken out half the sting of his disappointment. Let no man think lightly of the opinion of his wife in times of difficulty. Women have generally more acuteness of perception than men; and in moments of peril, or in circumstances that involve a crisis or turning-point in life, they have usually more resolution and greater instinctive judgment.

We recommend that every husband from the first should make his wife an allowance for ordinary household expenses—which he should pay weekly or monthly—and for the expenditure of which he should not, unless for some urgent reason, call her to account. A tolerably sure guide in estimating the amount of this item, which does not include rent, taxes, servants' wages, coals, or candles, etc., is to remember that in a small middle-class family, not exceeding *four*, the expense of each person for ordinary food amounts to fifteen shillings weekly; beyond that number to ten shillings weekly for each extra person, servant or otherwise. This estimate does not, of course, provide for wine or food of a luxurious kind. The largest establishment, indeed, may be safely calculated on the same scale.

A wife should also receive a stated allowance for dress, within which limit she ought always to restrict her expenses. Any excess of expenditure under this head should be left to the considerate kindness of her husband to concede. Nothing is more contemptible than for a woman to have perpetually to ask her husband for small sums for housekeeping expenses—

nothing more annoying and humiliating than to have to apply to him always for money for her own private use—nothing more disgusting than to see a man "molly-coddling" about marketing, and rummaging about for cheap articles of all kinds.

Let the husband beware, when things go wrong with him in business affairs, of venting his bitter feelings of disappointment and despair in the presence of his wife and family; feelings which, while abroad, he finds it practicable to restrain. It is as unjust as it is impolitic to indulge in such a habit.

A wife having married the man she loves above all others, must be expected in her turn to pay some court to him. Before marriage she has, doubtless, been made his idol. Every moment he could spare, and perhaps many more than he could properly so appropriate, have been devoted to her. How anxiously has he not revolved in his mind his worldly chances of making her happy! How often has he not had to reflect, before he made the proposal of marriage, whether he should be acting dishonorably towards her by incurring the risk, for the selfish motive of his own gratification, of placing her in a worse position than the one she occupied at home! And still more than this, he must have had to consider with anxiety the probability of having to provide for an increasing family, with all its concomitant expenses.

We say, then, that being married, and the honeymoon over, the husband must necessarily return to his usual occupations, which will, in all probability, engage the greater part of his thoughts, for he will now be desirous to have it in his power to procure various little indulgences for his wife's sake which he never would have dreamed of for his own. He comes to his home weary and fatigued; his young wife has had but her pleasures to gratify, or the quiet routine of her domestic duties to attend to, while he has been toiling through the day to enable her to gratify these pleasures and to fulfill these duties. Let, then, the dear, tired husband, at the close of his daily labors, be made welcome by the endearments of his loving spouse—let him be free from the care of having to satisfy the caprices of a petted wife. Let her now take her turn in paying those many little love-begotten attentions which married men look for to soothe them—let her reciprocate that devotion to herself, which, from the early hours of their love, he cherished for her, by her ever-ready endeavors to make him happy and his home attractive.

In the presence of other persons, however, married people should refrain from fulsome expressions of endearment to each other, the use of which, although a common practice, is really a mark of bad taste. It is desirable also to caution them against adopting the too prevalent vulgarism of calling each other, or indeed any person whatever, merely by the initial letter of their surname.

A married woman should always be very careful how she receives personal compliments. She should never court them, nor ever feel flattered by them, whether in her husband's presence or not. If in his presence, they can hardly fail to be distasteful to him; if in his absence, a lady, by a dignified demeanor, may always convince an assiduous admirer that his attentions are not well received, and at once and for ever stop all familiar advances. In case of insult, a wife should immediately make her husband acquainted therewith; as the only chance of safety to a villain lies in the concealment of such things by a lady from dread of consequences to her husband. From that moment he has her at advantage, and may very likely work on deliberately to the undermining of her character. He is thus enabled to play upon her fears, and taunt her with their mutual secret and its concealment, until she may be involved, guilelessly, in a web of apparent guilt, from which she can never extricate herself without risking the happiness of her future life.

Not the least useful piece of advice—homely though it be—that we can offer to newly-married ladies, is to remind them that husbands are men, and that men must eat. We can tell them, moreover, that men attach no small importance to this very essential operation, and that a very effectual way to keep them in good humor, as well as good condition, is for wives to study their husbands' peculiar likes and dislikes in this matter. Let the wife try, therefore, if she have not already done so, to get up a little knowledge of the art of *ordering* dinner, to say the least of it. This task, if she be disposed to learn it, will in time be easy enough; moreover, if in addition she should acquire some practical knowledge of cookery, she will find ample reward in the gratification it will be the means of affording her husband.

Servants are difficult subjects for a young wife to handle; she generally either spoils them by indulgence, or ruins them by finding fault unfairly. At last they either get the better of her, or she is voted too bad for them. The art lies in steady command and management of yourself as well as them.

An observance of the few following rules will in all probability insure a life of domestic harmony, peace, and comfort:—

To hear as little as possible whatever is to the prejudice of others; to believe nothing of the kind until you are compelled to admit the truth of it; never to take part in the circulation of evil report and idle gossip; always to moderate, as far as possible, harsh and unkind expressions reflecting upon others; always to believe that if the other side were heard, a very different account might be given of the matter.

In conclusion, we say emphatically to the newly-wedded wife, that attention to these practical hints will prolong her honeymoon throughout the whole period of wedded life, and cause her husband, as each year adds to the sum of his happiness, to bless the day when he first chose her as the nucleus round which he might consolidate the inestimable blessings of HOME.

> " How fair is home, in fancy's pictured theme,
> In wedded life, in love's romantic dream!
> Thence springs each hope, there every spring returns,
> Pure as the flame that upward, heavenward burns;
> There sits the wife, whose radiant smile is given—
> The daily sun of the domestic heaven;
> And when calm evening sheds a secret power,
> Her looks of love imparadise the hour;
> While children round, a beauteous train, appear,
> Attendant stars, revolving in her sphere."
>
> —HOLLAND's *Hopes of Matrimony.*

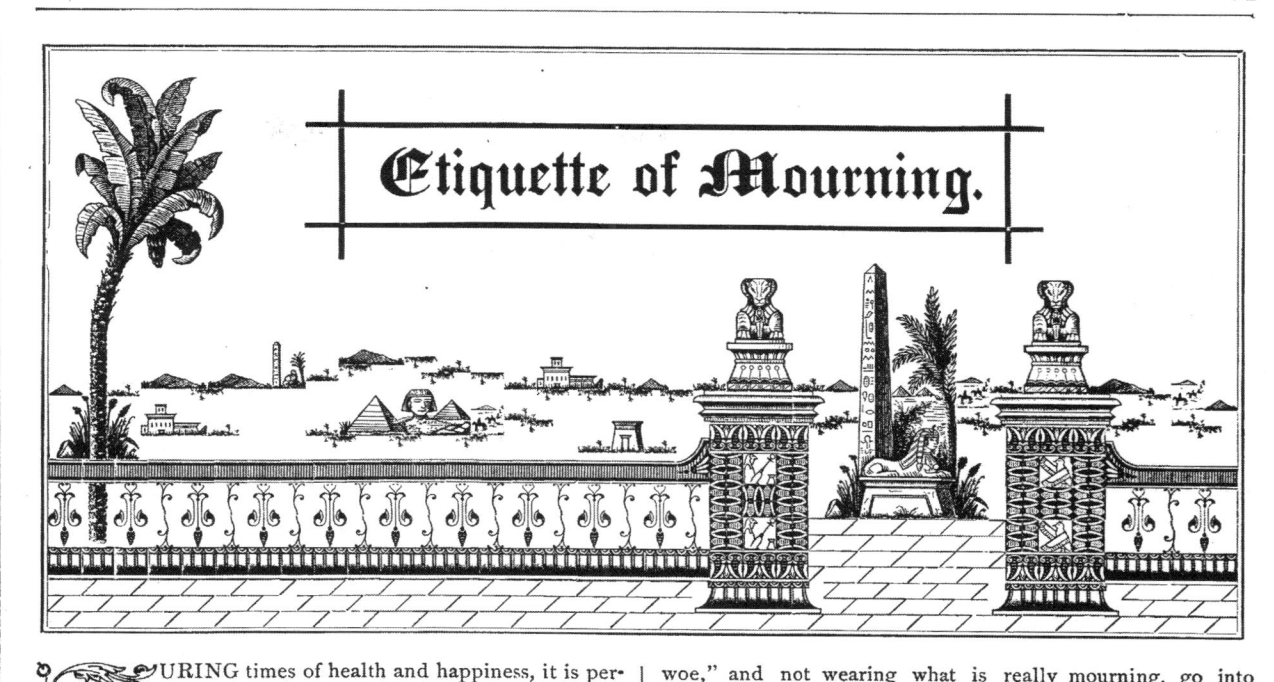

Etiquette of Mourning.

DURING times of health and happiness, it is perhaps rather trying to be asked to turn our thoughts into doleful channels; but sooner or later in our lives the sad time comes, for "Who breathes must suffer, and who thinks must mourn," and we have perforce to turn our minds to the inevitable and share "the common lot of man." In times of mourning it seems doubly hard to arouse ourselves, and allow the question of what to wear? to intrude itself. It is, however, necessary. Custom decrees, if even inclination does not prompt us, to show in some outward degree our respect for the dead by wearing the usual black.

We do not advise people to rush into black for every slight bereavement, nor, on the other hand, to show the utter disregard some do on the death of their relations, and only acknowledge the departure of those near and dear to them, by a band of crape round the arm. This is the mark of mourning adopted by those in the services who have to wear uniform, but hardly a fitting way of outwardly showing respect to the memory of those who have been called away from us, and whose loss we deplore. A short time since, a lady appeared in a new ruby satin dress, with a band of crape around her arm. The fact of the dress being new, showed that poverty did not cause this incongruity. It is hardly ever those who are styled "the poor," who err so against the accepted ideas of decency and respect. They always, however straitened they may be in circumstances, contrive to wear mourning for their deceased relatives. When black is fashionable, no difficulty is found in wearing it, and you meet all your friends so attired, but when it becomes a question of duty, these objections are raised as to the unnecessary expense, and the inconvenience of so dressing. The majority adhere in this respect to the customs their parents have followed; but the advanced few are those who air such sentiments, talk of the "mourning of the heart, not mere outward woe," and not wearing what is really mourning, go into society on the plea, "Oh! we know that those who are gone would not wish us to grieve for them." This may be all very well, but in the case of husbands, wives, parents, brothers, sisters, aunts, uncles, and the nearer-related cousins, decency
requires some outward mark of respect to their memory.

It will be as well to consider in succession the different degrees of mourning, and their duration.

The widow's is the deepest mourning of all. That old-fashioned material, bombazine, is now no longer heard of. Paramatta is in the most general use for widows. Barathea is also worn, but the first-named is the most frequently used for the first dresses; but, whatever the material, it is hidden by crape. The skirt, which is generally cut quite plain, and slightly trained, is completely covered with crape, put on quite plainly in one piece; the body and sleeves are also hidden with crape—the dress, in fact, presenting the appearance of one of crape. The body can be cut either *en princesse*, or have a deep jacket bodice; but whichever is preferred, crape should cover it completely.

The best and most economical crape for all wear is the rainproof crape, an improvement and development of the Albert crape, which is now brought to the greatest perfection of manufacture; it costs about half what ordinary crape does, to begin with, and is very much more durable; its imperviousness to weather being, of course, its great feature. The best make of this is quite suitable for widows' mourning. Its appearance equals that of much more expensive ordinary crape. We see no reason ourselves why, especially if economy be an object, the rainproof crape should not be worn for all degrees of mourning. We have no hesitation in advising it. For a second dress it would be a good plan to have some half-worn black dress entirely covered with crape—the rainproof crape—

this would save the better dress a little ; and as widows' first mourning is worn for a year and a day, it would be advisable to start with at least two dresses ; the crape on them could be renewed when necessary.

Widows' mantles are either made of silk or Paramatta, trimmed deeply with crape, or sometimes of Cyprus crape cloth, or cloth crape trimmed. The Cyprus crape cloth is a sort of crêpe material, and wears well, neither dust nor wet affecting it. In shape, the widow's mantle is a dolman, or long cape of good size ; this for elderly widows. For those younger, jackets or paletôts, crape-trimmed of course, are worn for winter wear, and for summer mantles made entirely of crape. The bonnet for first mourning is all of crape, with widow's cap tacked inside it, the small, close-fitting shape, with long crape veil hanging at the back ; besides this veil, a shorter one is worn over the face. Hats cannot be worn by widows, however young they might be, during the period of their deepest mourning.

The following list would be ample for a widow's outfit. We have given rather a large one because, of course, it can be curtailed as wished.

One best dress of Paramatta covered entirely with crape.

One dress, either a costume of Cyprus crape, or an old black dress covered with rainproof crape.

One Paramatta mantle lined with silk and deeply trimmed with crape.

One warmer jacket of cloth lined, trimmed with crape.

One bonnet of best silk crape, with long veil.

One bonnet of rainproof crape, with crape veil.

Twelve collars and cuffs of muslin or lawn, with deep hems. Several sets must be provided, say six of each kind.

One black stuff petticoat.

Four pairs of black hose, either silk, cashmere, or spun silk.

Twelve handkerchiefs with black borders for ordinary use, cambric.

Twelve of finer cambric for better occasions.

Caps, either of lisse, tulle, or tarlatan, shape depending very much on the age. Young widows wear chiefly the Marie Stuart shape, but all widows' caps have long streamers. They vary, of course, in price. Tarlatan are the easiest made at home, but we do not fancy home-made widows' caps are an economy, they soil so much more quickly than bought caps. It is a good plan to buy extra streamers and bows for them ; these can be made at home for the morning caps, very fine thread and needles being used for the work, which should be very fine, neat, and even. If in summer a parasol should be required, it should be of silk deeply trimmed with crape, almost covered with it, but no lace or fringe for the first year. Afterward mourning fringe might be put on. A muff, if required, would be made of Paramatta, and trimmed with crape.

The first mourning is worn for twelve months. Second mourning twelve months also ; the cap in second mourning is left off, and the crape no longer covers the dresses, but is put on in tucks. Elderly widows frequently remain in mourning for long periods, if not for the remainder of their lives, retaining the widow's cap, collar and cuffs, but leaving off the deep crape the second year, and afterwards entirely discarding crape, but wearing mourning materials such as Victoria cords, Janus cords, cashmere, and so on.

No ornaments are worn in such deep mourning, except jet, for the first year. Jet is, of course, allowable. Rich silk is, of course, admissible in widows' mourning, especially for evening wear, but it must always be deeply trimmed with crape for the first year, and the quantity afterwards gradually lessened. A silk costume is a very expensive item in a widow's mourning ; therefore we only allude to it—do not set it down as a necessity. The best silks for the purpose are rich, heavy silks, such as grosgrain, drap du nord, satin merveilleux. Furs are not admissible in widows' first mourning, though very dark sealskin and astrachan can be worn when the dress is changed. In other mournings, furs are now very generally worn—that is, after the first few months, but only dark furs.

Widows' lingerie, to be always nice, entails a considerable amount of expense. If collars, cuffs and caps are made at home, as we before said, they get soiled directly. As, however, it is not always possible to buy them when they require renewing, the following directions may prove of use : " Widow's cuffs, made in tarlatan, should be about nine inches long, according to the size of the wrist. They are not intended to overlap, but just to meet, fastened with two buttons and loops, placed near the upper and lower edges. The ordinary depth is five inches, with a wide hem at the top and bottom of an inch and a half depth. The material being merely a straight piece, they are easy to make. For the collar, the straight all-round shape, turning down over the collar of the dress, is the most usual. If any other shape is required, cut it in paper, and make it accordingly with the wide hem of one and a half inch. If the collar is straight, it will be merely necessary to turn it down; if rounded at all, it must be cut to the shape, run to the collar at the edge, and then turned down. Fine cotton and needles and neat work are required."

If an attempt is made to make widows' caps at home, first procure a good cap for a model, and copy it as exactly as possible. It must be made on a " dolly " or wooden block of a head, or it will never sit well.

To preserve widows' caps clean, fresh-looking, and of a good color, when not in use they should be put on cap-holders on a shelf in a cupboard, the long streamers turned up over the cap, and a piece of blue paper (thin) laid over them. So treated, they will with care last a long while, that, is, if there are two or three worn in turn, and they are put away in this manner when not in actual use.

It may be as well to sum up what we have said. Duration of mourning : Widow's first mourning lasts for a year and a day. Second mourning cap left off, less crape and silk for nine months (some curtail it to six), remaining three months of second year plain black without crape, and jet ornaments. At the end of the second year the mourning can be put off entirely ; but it is better taste to wear half mourning for at least six months longer ; and, as we have before mentioned, many widows never wear colors any more, unless for some solitary event, such as the wedding of a child, when they would probably put it off for the day. Materials :—

ETIQUETTE OF MOURNING.

Dresses and Mantles.—Paramatta, Barathea, silk trimmed with silk, Albert or rainproof crape.

Bonnets and Veils.—Crape.

Caps.—Lisse, tulle, tarlatan.

Collars and Cuffs.—Lawn and muslin.

Petticoats.—Black stuff or silk-quilted.

Pocket Handkerchiefs.—Cambric, black borders.

Hose.—Black Balbriggan, cashmere, or silk.

Gloves.—Black kid.

The mourning for parents ranks next to that of widows; for children by their parents, and for parents by their children, these being of course identical in degree. It lasts in either case twelve months—six months in crape trimmings, three in plain black, and three in half-mourning. It is, however, better taste to continue the plain black to the end of the year, and wear half-mourning for three months longer. Materials for first six months, either Paramatta, Barathea, or any of the black corded stuffs, such as Janus cord, about thirty-eight inches wide; Henrietta cord about same price and width. Such dresses would be trimmed with two deep tucks of crape, either Albert or rainproof, would be made plainly, the body trimmed with crape, and sleeves with deep crape cuffs. Collars and cuffs, to be worn during the first mourning would be made of muslin or lawn, with three or four tiny tucks in distinction to widows' with the wide, deep hem. Pocket handkerchiefs would be bordered with black. Black hose, silk or Balbriggan, would be worn, and black kid gloves. For out-door wear either a dolman mantle would be worn or a paletôt, either of silk or Paramatta, but in either case trimmed with crape. Crape bonnets or hats; if for young children, all crape for bonnets, hats, silk and crape; feathers (black) could be worn, and a jet clasp or arrow in the bonnet, but no other kind of jewelry is admissible but jet—that is, as long as crape is worn. Black furs, such as astrachan, may be worn, or very dark sealskin, or black sealskin cloth, now so fashionable, but no light furs of any sort. Silk dresses can be worn, crape-trimmed after the first three months if preferred, and if expense be no object; the lawn-tucked collars and cuffs would be worn with them. At the end of the six months crape can be put aside, and plain black, such as cashmere, worn, trimmed with silk if liked, but not satin, for that is not a mourning material, and is therefore never worn by those who strictly attend to mourning etiquette. With plain black, black gloves and hose would of course be worn, and jet, no gold or silver jewelry for at least nine months after the commencement of mourning; then, if the time expires in the twelve months, gray gloves might be worn, and gray ribbons, lace or plain linen collar and cuffs take the place of the lawn or muslin, and gray feathers might lighten the hat or bonnet, or reversible black and gray strings.

Many persons think it is in better taste not to commence half-mourning until after the expiration of a year, except in the case of young children, who are rarely kept in mourning beyond the twelve months.

A wife would wear just the same mourning for her husband's relations as for her own; thus, if her husband's mother died, she would wear mourning as deep as if for her own mother.

For Grandparents, the first mourning (crape) is worn for three months; second mourning, black, without crape, also worn for three months; and half-mourning for three more, or nine months in all. The same materials are worn, Paramatta, Barathea, various cords with crape and cashmere, and merino when the crape is left off.

For Sisters or Brothers, six months' mourning is usually worn. Crape for three, plain black for two, and half mourning for one month; the same sort of stuffs, the crape being put on in one deep tuck and two narrow tucks; bodice, crape trimmed; mantle or dolman, crape trimmed; bonnet of crape with feathers or jet, hat of silk and crape. Veil of hat with crape tuck, hose black silk, Balbriggan or cashmere, handkerchiefs black bordered. Silks can be worn after the first month if trimmed with crape.

For Uncles, Aunts, Nephews, or Nieces, crape is not worn, but plain black, with jet for three months.

For Great Uncles or Aunts, mourning would last for two months without crape.

For Cousins (first), six weeks are considered sufficient, three of which would be in half-mourning.

For Cousins less closely related, mourning is hardly ever put on unless they have been inmates of the house.

No invitations would be accepted before the funeral of any relatives closely enough related to you to put on mourning for. In the case of brothers, sisters, parents, and grandparents, society would be given up for at least three months, if not more, and it would be very bad taste to go to a ball or large festive gathering in crape. Widows do not enter society for at least a year—that is, during the period of their deepest mourning. With regard to *complimentary* mourning—as worn by mothers for the mother or father-in-law of their married children, black would be worn for six weeks or so without crape; by second wives for the parents of the first wife, for about three weeks, and in a few other cases.

It is better taste to wear mourning in making the first call after a bereavement on friends, but this is not a decided rule, only a graceful method of implying sympathy with those who are suffering affliction. But calls are not made until the cards with "thanks for kind inquiries" have been sent in return for the cards left at the time of decease. Letters of condolence should always be written on slightly black-edged paper, and it would be kind to intimate in the letter that no answer to it will be expected. Few realize the effort it is to those left to sit down and write answers to inquiries and letters, however kind and sympathizing they may have been.

Servants' Mourning.—Servants are not usually put into mourning except for the members of the household in which they are living, not for the relatives of their masters and mistresses, and very frequently only for the heads of the house, not for the junior members.

A best dress of Victoria cord or alpaca, two cotton dresses, black for mourning wear while at work. A cloth jacket, in case of master or mistress, with a slight crape trimming, a silk and crape bonnet, pair of black kid gloves, and some yards of black cap ribbon, would be the mourning given to the servants in the house at the time of the death of one of the heads of the establishment, and their mourning would be worn for at least six months, or even a year in some cases.

The following is a list of suitable materials for mourning of those relationships we have named, all of which can be obtained at any good mourning establishment.

Silk crape, Paramatta, Albert crape, Barathea, rainproof crape, silk, Cyprus crape. Janus cord, Victoria cord, Balmoral cloth, Cashmere Français, Kashgar Cashmere; these last are wide materials from 44 to 47 inches. Crape cloth looks precisely like crape, but is much lighter and cooler.

For summer wear drap d'été, a mixture of silk and wool, is suitable; barège for dinner dresses; nun's veil cloth, etc., etc.

The best all-black washing materials are cotton, satine, foulardine; black and white for slighter mourning, black with tiny white spots or sprigs.

Children should be dressed in these black washing materials—that is, for summer wear, in preference to the thicker materials, as for young children, crape is soon dispensed with. Neither velvet, satin, nor plush can be worn in mourning—that is in strict mourning—for they are not mourning materials. Attempts have been made to bring in some colors, such as red or violet, and we consider them suitable to slight mourning; but the only color really admissible for half-mourning is gray, or the palest lavender, gray gloves sewn with black, gray and black reversible ribbons, gray and black feathers, gray flowers mixed with black, and so on.

In all cases of mourning it is the best plan to write to some well-known house for patterns; good mourning establishments can afford to sell better materials at cheaper rates than small, inferior houses. Large firms have always a good choice of materials for mourning on hand; and it is really far greater economy to buy good materials when going into mourning, than cheap flimsy stuffs, which give no wear at all; besides, such houses send out books of fashions and prices for making up mourning costumes, which give a good idea of the expense to be incurred, even if it is not found cheaper to purchase and have mourning made up by them.

Mourning has generally to be purchased hurriedly, and too often a dressmaker gets *carte blanche* almost to furnish the mourning. If such is the case, no wonder mourning is considered expensive; for things which are quite unnecessary, such as expensive crape in the place of rainproof kinds, more crape used than the degre of mourning requires, and many extravagancies of a like nature, naturally swell such a bill into one of large proportions, when by a little forethought the necessary black could have been purchased at a far more reasonable rate.

It is not necessary to have very expensive mourning if our means will not allow it; we should learn to suit our requirement to the state of our purses. But we sincerely trust the old custom of wearing decent mourning for those taken away from us, will never be really discontinued in America, for it is one of those proofs of our home affections which can never be done away with without a loss of national respect.

Golden Rules of Etiquette.

INTRODUCTIONS.

SHAKING hands after an introduction has taken place is merely optional not necessary.

It is not necessary to introduce people who meet at your house on morning calls.

It is optional after such an introduction, with the parties introduced, to continue or drop the acquaintance so formed.

A friend visiting at your house must be introduced to all callers, who are bound to continue the acquaintance as long as the friend is your guest.

A gentleman must always raise his hat, if introduced in the street, to either lady or gentleman.

Letters of introduction to and from business men, for business purposes, may be delivered by the bearers in person, and etiquette does not require the receiver to entertain the person introduced as the private friend of the writer.

BALL.

A hundred gents or over that number constitute a ball. The lady of the house must stand near the door, so as to receive her guests, to each of whom she must find something to say, no matter how trifling. The host must also be near, to welcome arrivals, and the sons to introduce people. The young ladies and their very intimate friends must see that the dances are kept up, and should not dance themselves till they have found partners for all their friends. They may with perfect propriety ask any gentleman present to be introduced to a partner, and he is bound to accept the invitation; but the lady must be careful whom she asks. Some young ladies do not dance at all, preferring to see their friends amused, and for fear of causing jealousies.

If you escort a lady to a ball, call for her at the appointed hour, in a carriage, and send a bouquet early in the day. Upon arriving at the house where the ball is held, escort your charge to the dressing-room door. She may or may not dance the first dance with you. Ask her. You must see that she gets her supper, and offer to leave the ball at any hour that she may be desirous of so doing.

No gentleman should wait for the "fiddles to strike up" to engage a partner.

At a public ball, a lady may refuse to have a gentleman presented to her.

Do not remain too late.

"May I have the pleasure of the waltz or quadrille with you," is all that a gentleman need say on introduction. If the lady says yes, he asks permission to write his name on her card.

Always give your arm to a lady in crossing a ball-room.

Do not feel offended if your fair partner fails to bow to you when you meet her after a ball. It is optional; some young ladies are very timid, and fear that gentlemen forget them.

Do not feel slighted if your fair companion does not invite you to enter her home on returning from the ball. If she does invite you, decline.

AT HOMES—RECEPTIONS—GIVING PARTIES.

Parties in cities consist of—at homes, receptions, conversaziones, private concerts, private theatricals, soirées, dramatic tea-parties, matinées, or a gathering of people.

In the country, the in-door parties comprise small dancing-parties, tea-parties, and conversaziones; but the out-door occasions are of much greater number and variety; lawn-tennis parties, croquet, sailing, and boating parties, picnics, private fêtes, berrying parties, nutting parties, May festivals, Fourth of July festivals, anything for a day spent in out-door frolic.

For "Receptions" and "At Homes," and conversaziones invitations should be sent out a week beforehand.

At a reception you have music and singing, perhaps recitations. Light refreshments are served, and the hostess makes the most of her rooms in display, etc.

Gentlemen should take elderly ladies into refreshments.

Let amateur performers learn something off by heart. Being provided with notes is not stylish.

Let no person offer to turn over the leaves of a music book for a performer, unless he or she can read music rapidly.

If you play an accompaniment show off the singer not yourself.

If you get up private theatricals, secure the best amateur talent.

Be punctual at lawn-tennis and croquet parties.

Gentlemen at picnics must turn into waiters for the *nonce*, and look to the appetites of the ladies.

SALUTATIONS.

Do not insult by offering two fingers when shaking hands.

Remove your right hand glove in the street; retain it in the house.

Do not wring off the wrist of the person with whom you shake hands.

The lady recognizes the gentleman first by bowing. The gentleman must wait till he is bowed to by the lady.

When a lady is desirous of ending a conversation in the street she should bow slightly, and the gentleman must instantly take his leave.

If the lady " proceeds upon her way " without breaking up conversation, then the gentleman is bound to join her in the promenade.

At home, the lady extends her hand to every guest.

A gentleman is at liberty to bow to a lady seated at a window, but if he is in the window he is not to bow to a lady in the street.

The gentleman never offers to shake hands with the lady. It is her prerogative to stretch forth her hand to his.

A gentleman may at all times bow to a lady he may meet on a stairway, even if not acquainted. If at the foot of the stairs, he must bow, pass her and ascend before her. If at the head of the stairs, he must bow, and wait for her to precede him in the descent.

If a gentleman is walking with a friend, and the friend bows to a lady, he is bound to bow although he may be unacquainted with the lady.

CALLS.

If a lady has a particular day set aside for receiving callers, call on that day *only*.

You can make a formal call in the morning, a friendly one in the evening.

Gentlemen may call in the morning on the following excuses:—

After a breakfast, luncheon, dinner, reception, or ball.

On the occasion of any joy or grief.

After escorting a lady on the previous evening.

Be prompt on the first call.

In the morning, call after ten o'clock; in the evening, not later than eight.

In the evening informal call leave hat, coat, umbrella, cane, and overshoes in the hall.

If you find your host or hostess attired for going out, beat a hasty retreat.

Never put anything but your name and address on your card when making a social call. Thus:—

John Smith

295 Fifth Avenue, N. Y.

𝔐𝔞𝔯𝔱𝔦𝔫 𝔅𝔲𝔯𝔨𝔢, 𝔐. 𝔇.,

128 Lexington Avenue, N. Y.

Captain Geyer Copinger,

U. S. A.

𝔏𝔦𝔢𝔲𝔱𝔢𝔫𝔞𝔫𝔱 𝔍𝔬𝔰𝔢𝔭𝔥 𝔉𝔩𝔦𝔫𝔱.

U. S. N.

GOLDEN RULES OF ETIQUETTE.

Never consult your watch before taking your departure.

Leave a card before departing for the country or Europe with the words P. P. C. (*Pour Pendre Congé.* To Take Leave) on the left hand corner in pencil.

Leave a card during the illness of your friend.

Leave a card the day after a ball or big dinner party.

After a small party leave a card within a week. Wives leave the cards of their husbands.

The first callers are the residents in the place.

Call upon the gent who comes to stay with your friend.

Do not keep your callers waiting.

Do not remove your gloves when making a formal call.

No callers should fiddle with books, pictures, albums, window-blinds, etc.

When you call on a friend at a hotel or boarding-house write his or her name above your own on *your own card*.

DINNER.

Gentlemen should stand behind their respective chairs until all the ladies are seated, and then take their own seats. Care should be taken that their chairs do not stand upon the dresses of the ladies beside them.

Grace is said by a clergyman, if there is one present, if not, by the host. The clergyman should be invited to say grace by the host. People usually stand till grace is over.

If the dinner is *à la Russe*, the carving will be done behind a screen. Keep your servants from making a noise behind the screen.

Always say "thanks," or "thank you," to the servant or waiter.

Never decline wine by clapping your hand on top of your glass.

Do not eat ravenously.

Do not smack the lips.

Never take a long, deep breath after you finish eating, as if you were tired eating.

Make no noises in your mouth or throat.

Do not suck your teeth or roll your tongue around the outside of your gums.

Never, no NEVER, NEVER, put your knife into your mouth.

Do not pick your teeth, or plunge your finger into your mouth.

Do not spit out fish-bones upon your plate.

Never take the bones of fowl or birds up in your fingers to gnaw or suck them. Remove the meat with your knife, and convey it to your mouth with your fork. Do not polish or scrape the bone.

Wipe your finger-tips upon the table napkin.

Do not use the tablecloth to wipe your mouth.

Do not either praise or dispraise what is placed before you.

Do not drink or speak when you have anything in your mouth.

When you are helped begin to eat.

Never watch the dishes as they are uncovered, or cry out when you perceive something dainty.

Do not attempt to tuck your napkin, bib fashion, into your shirt collar. Unfold it partially and place it in your lap, covering your knees. A lady may slip a corner under her belt if there is danger of its falling upon her dress.

Do not talk loudly. Do not whisper. Do not laugh too loudly.

Use the table articles, such as spoon, butter-knife, etc., etc.

Never clean your plate. Leave something on it.

Never attempt to propose a toast or sentiment, at all events till the dessert is well over. We have seen men attempt this before the roasts appeared.

Take chablis with your oysters or clams.

Take sherry with your soup.

Take champagne with the entrées.

Take Burgundy with game.

Take port with cheese.

Take claret after dessert.

Take a *pousse café*, a liqueur, after coffee.

Never spit the skins of grapes, the stones or pips of fruits. Receive them upon the prongs of your fork, laid horizontally, and place them as best you can upon the edge of your plate.

Do not play with your fingers upon the table.

Do not play with your knife and fork, fidget with your salt-cellar, balance your spoon on your tumbler, or make pills of your bread.

Do not illustrate your anecdotes by plans drawn upon the table with your nail.

Do not stretch your feet out under the table, so as to touch those of your opposite neighbor.

Do not tilt your chair.

Endeavor to take an easy position at table, neither pressing too closely up to it, nor yet so far away as to risk depositing your food upon the floor.

Give your neighbor as much elbow room as possible.

If the dinner is for gentlemen guests alone, and the lady of the house presides, her duties are over when she rises after dessert. The gentlemen do not expect to see her again. Cigars may be served with the coffee, and then the servants may retire.

In case of a stag party, like this, the lady of the house is much better away. Then the *oldest* friend of the host takes her seat.

BAPTISM.

Let the godfather and godmother be of the same church as the child that is to be baptized.

Never refuse to stand sponsor without good cause.

The godmother should select the godfather.

The godparents should make the infant a present, a silver cup, or a set consisting of knife, fork and spoon.

Very young persons should not be asked to become sponsors.

The nurse carrying the child enters the church first, then come the sponsors, then the happy father, and the guests.

The sponsors stand thus: godfather on the right of the child; godmother on the left.

The sponsors bow when the clergyman asks who the sponsors are.

Do not offer to act as sponsors. The parents make the selection.

Praise the baby under all circumstances.

FUNERALS.

Do not speak loudly in the house of mourning. Do not ask to see the members of the bereaved family. Invitations are printed, and in this form:—

You are respectfully invited to attend the funeral of Mr. John Smith on Friday, June 28, 1882, at 9 o'clock a. m., from his late residence, 148 West 68th Street. To proceed to Cyprus Grove Cemetery,

If the services are at church:—

You are respectfully invited to attend the funeral of Mr. John Smith, from the Church of the Nativity, Madison Avenue, on Friday, June 28th, at 9 o'clock a. m. To proceed to Cyprus Grove Cemetery.

No further notice need be sent, if the invitation is given through the newspapers.

Do not go to the house of your dead friend until the hour named. The last moments are, indeed, precious to the grief-stricken relatives.

The clergyman leaves the house first, and enters the carriage that precedes the hearse; the coffin comes next; then come the relatives.

Do not salute the relatives.

The master of the ceremonies assists at the carriages, also at the church.

Hats must be removed as the coffin passes from the hearse to the church, and from the church to the hearse, and a double line formed.

Wear black clothes, or as near to that color as may be.

Send a carriage for the clergyman.

Send only white flowers, and on the morning of the funeral.

Pall-bearers must be the immediate friends of the deceased.

Gloves and crape, if given, must be presented as the gentlemen enter the house.

Leave cards for the family of the deceased during the week following the obsequies. The proper person to purchase mourning is the nearest lady friend of the family.

No member of the family of the deceased shall be seen out-of-doors till after the funeral.

HOTELS.

Ladies traveling alone will request the escort of a waiter from the dining-room door to the table.

Ladies will make up their minds quickly as to what dishes they propose to order.

Ladies will accept table civilities from gentlemen, such as passing salt, etc., etc.

The piano of the hotel is public property, but a lady should be careful about monopolizing it.

Ladies will not linger in the hall, and will avoid the public entrance.

Recognition across the dining-room is not required.

AMUSEMENTS.

Gentlemen will always invite another lady to accompany a young lady in taking her for the *first time* to a place of amusement.

Give the ladies as long a notice as possible.

A lady does not bow across a theater, a gentleman does

Do not arrive late at any entertainment.

No lady stares round a theater with an opera glass.

During the performance speak in a low tone.

The gentleman walks before the lady until he reaches the seat, then he bows her into her seat.

Never leave the lady alone.

Never stand in the way of others in picture galleries.

It is permissible for a gentleman to join ladies for a moment or two between the acts.

Be careful to enter a place of amusement as quietly and unostentatiously as possible.

Never laugh loudly, and if you applaud, do so earnestly, but not too energetically.

BY BOAT AND RAIL.

Ladies will not permit their escorts to enter any apartment reserved for ladies only.

Ladies traveling alone should consult conductors or captains.

Ladies will thank gentlemen who raise or lower windows, coldly but politely.

If a person crushes or crowds you, and apologizes, accept the apology by a cold bow.

Gentlemen escorts must pay the most delicate and earnest care to the lady or ladies under their care. The attention must be unremitting.

At a hotel, the escort must see to everything, rooms, etc., etc.

Courtesies in traveling are always *en règle*, but there must be no attempt at familiarity.

Gentlemen will commence conversations.

Gentlemen will assist ladies to alight from the cars.

A gentleman may offer to escort a lady to the refreshment saloon.

A gentleman may offer his newspaper.

THE STREET.

Ladies bow first to gentlemen. The gentleman so saluted lifts his hat and bows.

Gentlemen will offer to carry parcels for ladies.

Gentlemen will not smoke when walking with ladies.

Candy or bananas, or anything else, should not be eaten in the street.

Ladies and old gentlemen are given the portion of the sidewalk next to the houses.

Ladies should not walk too rapidly.

Ladies may accept umbrella assistance from male friends and acquaintances, but from strangers never.

In crossing through a narrow place, or across a plank, or in-doors, or up-stairs, the lady goes first.

A gentleman may assist a lady to cross a puddle or across a crowded street.

A gentleman should never let a lady stand in a railway car, a street car, a stage, or a ferry-boat, if he has a seat to offer her. A man remaining seated while a woman stands, is absolutely hoggish.

A gentleman will pass a lady's fare in a street car or stage.

No lady will salute across a street.

A very stiff bow gives the "cut."

Young people must wait for recognition from their elders.

Gentlemen will open store, and all other doors for ladies to pass, lifting hat at same time.

Do not bow from a store to a person in the street.

VISITS.

"You'll come and see me some time," is no invitation. Recollect this!

If you are asked by letter to make a visit, reply instanter.

If you are asked to visit friends for any period, write at once and name the time most convenient to yourself.

Hosts should always have a guest room, and special care should be given to it. It should be warmed in winter and cooled in summer. Its comforts should be made a study.

Hosts should either meet or send to the depot for their guests. The baggage should be looked after, and any trouble spared the person invited.

If the guest arrives in the morning, special breakfast should be prepared; if at night, special supper. If the guest is delicate or a late riser, special meals should be prepared.

Guests will conform as much as possible to the habits of their hosts.

Hosts will amuse their guests as much as possible, by entertainments, by taking them to places of interest, and by introductions to entertaining people.

The hostess need not appear between breakfast and luncheon. She has her household duties to attend to.

No guest will make an outside engagement without consulting the host.

Hosts will accept no invitations that do not include their guests.

Guests should bring their own writing materials, sewing materials, wools, etc., etc. Ladies should volunteer to assist the hostess in sewing, etc.

Guests may use the servants as if they were their own, but always in reason.

If a guest injures anything in the house at which he or she may be stopping, such as a glass bowl, a painting, etc., etc., he or she will repair the loss by sending an article similar to that which has been injured.

Gentlemen may send gifts of flowers, candies, bonbons, etc.; and guests may always present the baby with a gift.

Do not open any letters delivered to you in the presence of your host and hostess without saying, "Have I your permission?" Hosts will do the same toward their guests.

No lady guest pays for anything, carriage, boat, car, etc.

Hosts, when their guests are about to leave, will see that the baggage is cared for, and will leave the guest at the depot or boat.

THE LANGUAGE OF FLOWERS.

HOW the universal heart of man blesses flowers! They are wreathed round the cradle, the marriage-altar, and the tomb. The Persian in the far East delights in their perfume, and writes his love in nosegays; while the Indian child of the far West claps his hands with glee as he gathers the abundant blossoms, — the illuminated scriptures of the prairies. The Cupid of the ancient Hindoos tipped his arrows with flowers, and orange-flowers are a bridal crown with us, a nation of yesterday. Flowers garlanded the Grecian altar, and hung in votive wreath before the Christian shrine. All these are appropriate uses. Flowers should deck the brow of the youthful bride, for they are in themselves a lovely type of marriage. They should twine round the tomb, for their perpetually renewed beauty is a symbol of the resurrection. They should festoon the altar, for their fragrance and their beauty ascend in perpetual worship before the Most High.

Flowers have a language of their own, and it is this bright particular language that we would teach our readers. How charmingly a young gentleman can speak to a young lady, and with what eloquent silence in this delightful language. How delicately she can respond, the beautiful little flowers telling her tale in perfumed words; what a delicate story the myrtle or the rose tells! How unhappy that which basil, or the yellow rose reveals, while ivy is the most faithful of all.

ALMOND—HOPE.

The hope, in dreams of a happier hour,
That alights upon misery's brow,
Springs out of the silvery almond flower,
That blooms on a leafless bough.

Abecedary ....Volubility.
Abatina ....Fickleness.
Acacia ....Friendship.
Acacia, Rose or White ...Elegance.
Acacia, Yellow............Secret love.
Acanthus ....The fine arts. Artifice.
Acalia ....Temperance.
Achillea Millefolia.......War.
Aconite (Wolfsbane).....Misanthropy.
Aconite, Crowfoot.......Luster.
Adonis, Flos..............Painful recollections
African Marigold........Vulgar minds.
Agnus Castus............Coldness. Indifference.
Agrimony................Thankfulness. Gratitude.
Almond (Common).......Stupidity. Indiscretion.
Almond (Flowering).....Hope.
Almond, Laurel..........Perfidy.
Allspice...................Compassion.
Aloe ....Grief. Religious superstition.
Althæa Frutex (Syrian Mallow)................Persuasion.
Alyssum (Sweet) ....Worth beyond beauty.
Amaranth (Globe) ....Immortality. Unfading love.
Amaranth (Cockscomb)..Foppery. Affectation.
Amaryllis ....Pride. Timidity. Splendid beauty.
Ambrosia ....Love returned.
American Cowslip.......Divine beauty.
American Elm...........Patriotism.
American Linden........Matrimony.
American Starwort......Welcome to a stranger. Cheerfulness in old age.
Amethyst ....Admiration.

THE LANGUAGE OF FLOWERS.

Anemone (Zephyr Flower)Sickness. Expectation.
Anemone (Garden)......Forsaken.
Angelica................Inspiration.
Angrec.................Royalty.
Apple..................Temptation.
Apple (Blossom)........Preference. Fame speaks him great and good.
Apple, Thorn...........Deceitful charms.
Apocynum (Dog's Vane).Deceit.
Arbor Vitæ.............Unchanging friendship. Live for me.
Arum (Wake Robin).....Ardor.
Ash-leaved Trumpet Flower................Separation.
Ash Tree...............Grandeur.
Aspen Tree.............Lamentation.
Aster (China)..........Variety. Afterthought.
Asphodel...............My regrets follow you to the grave.
Auricula...............Painting.
Auricula, Scarlet.......Avarice.
Austurtium.............Splendor.
Azalea.................Temperance.

Bachelor's Buttons......Celibacy.
Balm...................Sympathy.
Balm, Gentle...........Pleasantry.
Balm of Gilead.........Cure. Relief.
Balsam, Red............Touch me not. Impatient resolves.
Balsam, Yellow.........Impatience.
Barberry...............Sourness of temper.
Barberry Tree..........Sharpness.
Basil..................Hatred.
Bay Leaf...............I change but in death.
Bay (Rose) Rhododendron.................Danger. Beware.
Bay Tree...............Glory.
Bay Wreath.............Reward of merit.
Bearded Crepis.........Protection.
Beech Tree.............Prosperity.
Bee Orchis.............Industry.
Bee Ophrys.............Error.
Belladonna.............Silence.
Bell Flower, Pyramidal..Constancy.
Bell Flower (small white) Gratitude.
Belvedere..............I declare against you
Betony.................Surprise.
Bilberry...............Treachery.
Bindweed, Great........Insinuation.
Bindweed, Small........Humility.
Birch..................Meekness.
Birdsfoot, Trefoil......Revenge.
Bittersweet; Nightshade.Truth.
Black Poplar...........Courage.
Blackthorn.............Difficulty.
Bladder Nut Tree.......Frivolity. Amusement.
Bluebottle (Century)....Delicacy.
Bluebell...............Constancy.
Blue-flowered Greek Valerian.................Rupture.
Bonus Henricus.........Goodness.
Borage.................Bluntness.
Box Tree...............Stoicism.
Bramble................Lowliness. Envy. Remorse.
Branch of Currants.....You please all.

Branch of Thorns.......Severity. Rigor.
Bridal Rose............Happy love.
Broom..................Humility. Neatness
Buckbean...............Calm repose.
Bud of White Rose......Heart ignorant of love.
Bugloss................Falsehood.
Bulrush................Indiscretion. Docility.
Bundle of Reeds, with their Panicles..........Music.
Burdock................Importunity. Touch me not.
Buttercup (Kingcup)....Ingratitude. Childishness.
Butterfly Orchis........Gaiety.
Butterfly Weed.........Let me go.

Cabbage................Profit.
Cacalia................Adulation.
Cactus.................Warmth.
Calla Æthiopica........Magnificent Beauty.
Calycanthus............Benevolence.
Camellia Japonica, Red..Unpretending excellence.
Camellia Japonica, White.Perfected loveliness.
Camomile...............Energy in adversity.
Canary Grass...........Perseverance.
Candytuft..............Indifference.
Canterbury Bell........Acknowledgment.
Cape Jasmine...........I'm too happy.
Cardamine..............Paternal error.
Carnation, Deep Red....Alas! for my poor heart.
Carnation, Striped.....Refusal.
Carnation, Yellow......Disdain.
Cardinal Flower........Distinction.
Catchfly...............Snare.
Catchfly, Red..........Youthful love.
Catchfly, White........Betrayed.
Cedar..................Strength.
Cedar of Lebanon.......Incorruptible.
Cedar Leaf.............I live for thee.
Celandine (Lesser).....Joys to come.
Century................Delicacy.
Cereus (Creeping)......Modest genius.
Champignon.............Suspicion.
Chequered Fritillary...Persecution.
Cherry Tree............Good education.
Cherry Tree, White.....Deception.
Chestnut Tree..........Do me justice. Luxury.
Chickweed..............Rendezvous.
Chicory................Frugality.
China Aster............Variety.
China Aster, Double....I partake your sentiments.
China Aster, Single....I will think of it.
China or Indian Pink...Aversion.
China Rose.............Beauty always new.
Chinese Chrysanthemum.Cheerfulness under adversity.
Christmas Rose.........Relieve my anxiety.
Chrysanthemum, Red....I love.
Chrysanthemum, White..Truth.
Chrysanthemum, Yellow.Slighted love.
Cinquefoil.............Maternal affection.
Circæa.................Spell.
Cistus, or Rock Rose...Popular favor.
Cistus, Gum............I shall die tomorrow.
Citron.................Ill-natured beauty.

Clematis...............Mental beauty.
Clematis, Evergreen....Poverty.
Clotbur................Rudeness. Pertinacity.
Cloves.................Dignity.
Clover, Four-leaved....Be mine.
Clover, Red............Industry.
Clover, White..........Think of me.
Cobæa..................Gossip.
Cockscomb Amaranth....Foppery. Affectation. Singularity.
Colchicum, or Meadow Saffron................My best days are past.
Coltsfoot..............Justice shall be done
Columbine..............Folly.
Columbine, Purple......Resolved to win.
Columbine, Red.........Anxious and trembling.
Convolvulus............Bonds.
Convolvulus, Blue(Minor)Repose. Night.
Convolvulus, Major.....Extinguished hopes.
Convolvulus, Pink......Worth sustained by judicious and tender affection.
Corchorus..............Impatient of absence.
Coreopsis..............Always cheerful.
Coreopsis Arkansa......Love at first sight.
Coriander..............Hidden worth.
Corn...................Riches.
Corn, Broken...........Quarrel.
Corn Straw.............Agreement.
Corn Bottle............Delicacy.
Corn Cockle............Gentility.
Cornel Tree............Duration.
Coronella..............Success crown your wishes.
Cowslip................Pensiveness. Winning grace.
Cowslip, American......Divine beauty. You are my divinity.
Cranberry..............Cure for heartache.
Creeping Cereus........Horror.
Cress..................Stability. Power.
Crocus.................Abuse not.
Crocus, Spring.........Youthful gladness.
Crocus, Saffron........Mirth.
Crown Imperial.........Majesty. Power.
Crowsbill..............Envy.
Crowfoot...............Ingratitude.
Crowfoot (Aconiteleaved) Luster.
Cocoa Plant............Ardor.
Cudweed, American......Unceasing remembrance.
Currant................Thy frown will kill me.
Cuscuta................Meanness.
Cyclamen...............Diffidence.
Cypress................Death. Mourning.

DAFFODIL—REGARD.

I.

Fair Daffodils, we weep to see
  You haste away so soon ;
As yet the early-rising sun
  Has not attained his noon ;
    Stay, stay,
  Until the hastening day
    Has run
  But to the even song,
And, having prayed together, we
  Will go with you along.

THE LANGUAGE OF FLOWERS.

II.

We have short time to stay as ye,
We have as fleet a spring,
As quick a growth to meet decay
As you or anything;
We die
As your hours do, and dry
Away,
Like to the summer's rain,
Or as the pearls of morning's dew,
Ne'er to be found again.

Daffodil...................Regard.
Dahlia....................Instability.
Daisy.....................Innocence.
Daisy, Garden............I share your sentiments.
Daisy, Michaelmas........Farewell.
Daisy, Party-colored.....Beauty.
Daisy, Wild..............I will think of it.
Damask Rose..............Brilliant complexion
Dandelion................Rustic oracle.
Daphne, Odora............Painting the lily.
Darnel (Ray grass).......Vice.
Dead Leaves..............Sadness.
Dew Plant................A serenade.
Dittany of Crete.........Birth.
Dittany of Crete, White..Passion.
Dock.....................Patience.
Dodder of Thyme..........Baseness.
Dogsbane.................Deceit. Falsehood.
Dogwood..................Durability.
Dragon Plant.............Snare.
Dragonwort...............Horror.
Dried Flax...............Utility.

Ebony Tree...............Blackness.
Eglantine (Sweetbrier)...Poetry. I wound to heal.
Elder....................Zealousness.
Elm......................Dignity.
Enchanter's Nightshade...Witchcraft. Sorcery.
Endive...................Frugality.
Eupatorium...............Delay.
Everflowering Candytuft..Indifference.
Evergreen Clematis.......Poverty.
Evergreen Thorn..........Solace in adversity.
Everlasting..............Never-ceasing remembrance.
Everlasting Pea..........Lasting pleasure.

Fennel...................Worthy of all praise. Strength.
Fern.....................Fascination.
Ficoides, Ice Plant......Your looks freeze me.
Fig......................Argument.
Fig Marigold.............Idleness.
Fig Tree.................Prolific.
Filbert..................Reconciliation.
Fir......................Time.
Fir Tree.................Elevation.
Flax.....................Domestic industry. Fate. I feel your kindness.
Flax-leaved Goldy-locks..Tardiness.
Fleur-de-Lis.............Flame. I burn.
Fleur-de-Luce............Fire.
Flowering Fern...........Reverie.
Flowering Reed...........Confidence in Heaven.
Flower-of-an-Hour........Delicate beauty.

Fly Orchis...............Error.
Flytrap..................Deceit.
Fool's Parsley...........Silliness.
Forget Me Not............True love. Forget me not.
Foxglove.................Insincerity.
Foxtail Grass............Sporting.
French Honeysuckle.......Rustic beauty.
French Marigold..........Jealousy.
French Willow............Bravery and humanity.
Frog Ophrys..............Disgust.
Fuller's Teasel..........Misanthropy.
Fumitory.................Spleen.
Fuschia, Scarlet.........Taste.

Garden Anemone...........Forsaken.
Garden Chervil...........Sincerity.
Garden Daisy.............I partake your sentiments.
Garden Marigold..........Uneasiness.
Garden Ranunculus........You are rich in attractions.
Garden Sage..............Esteem.
Garland of Roses.........Reward of virtue.
Germander Speedwell......Facility.
Geranium, Dark...........Melancholy.
Geranium, Ivy............Bridal favor.
Geranium, Lemon..........Unexpected meeting.
Geranium, Nutmeg.........Expected meeting.
Geranium, Oak-leaved.....True friendship
Geranium, Penciled.......Ingenuity.
Geranium, Rose-scented...Preference.
Geranium, Scarlet........Comforting. Stupidity.
Geranium, Silver-leaved..Recall.
Geranium, Wild...........Steadfast piety.
Gilliflower..............Bonds of affection.
Glory Flower.............Glorious beauty.
Goat's Rue...............Reason.
Golden Rod...............Precaution.
Gooseberry...............Anticipation.
Gourd....................Extent. Bulk.
Grape, Wild..............Charity.
Grass....................Submission. Utility.
Guelder Rose.............Winter. Age.

Hand Flower Tree.........Warning.
Harebell.................Submission. Grief.
Hawkweed.................Quicksightedness.
Hawthorn.................Hope.
Hazel....................Reconciliation.
Heath....................Solitude.
Helenium.................Tears.
Heliotrope...............Devotion. Faithfulness.
Hellebore................Scandal. Calumny.
Helmet Flower (Monkshood)..Knight-errantry.
Hemlock..................You will be my death.
Hemp.....................Fate.
Henbane..................Imperfection.
Hepatica.................Confidence.
Hibiscus.................Delicate beauty.
Holly....................Foresight.
Holly Herb...............Enchantment.
Hollyhock................Ambition. Fecundity.
Honesty..................Honesty. Fascination.

Honey Flower.............Love, sweet and secret.
Honeysuckle..............Generous and devoted affection.
Honeysuckle (Coral)......The color of my fate.
Honeysuckle (French).....Rustic beauty.
Hop......................Injustice.
Hornbean.................Ornament.
Horse Chestnut...........Luxury.
Hortensia................You are cold.
Houseleek................Vivacity. Domestic industry.
Houstonia................Content.
Hoya.....................Sculpture.
Humble Plant.............Despondency.
Hundred-leaved Rose......Dignity of mind.
Hyacinth.................Sport. Game. Play.
Hyacinth, White..........Unobtrusive loveliness.
Hydrangea................A boaster. Heartlessness.
Hyssop...................Cleanliness.

Iceland Moss.............Health.
Ice Plant................Your looks freeze me.
Imperial Montague........Power.
Indian Cress.............Warlike trophy.
Indian Jasmine (Ipomœa)..Attachment.
Indian Pink (Double).....Always lovely.
Indian Plum..............Privation.
Iris.....................Message.
Iris German..............Flame.
Ivy......................Fidelity. Marriage.
Ivy, Sprig of, with tendrils..Assiduous to please.

Jacob's Ladder...........Come down.
Japan Rose...............Beauty is your only attraction.
Jasmine..................Amiability.
Jasmine, Cape............Transport of joy.
Jasmine, Carolina........Separation.
Jasmine, Indian..........I attach myself to you.
Jasmine, Spanish.........Sensuality.
Jasmine, Yellow..........Grace and elegance.
Jonquil..................I desire a return of affection.
Judas Tree...............Unbelief. Betrayal
Juniper..................Succor. Protection.
Justicia.................The perfection of female loveliness.

Kennedia.................Mental beauty.
King-cups................Desire of riches.

Laburnum.................Forsaken. Pensive beauty.
Lady's Slipper...........Capricious beauty. Win me and wear me.
Lagerstræmia, Indian.....Eloquence.
Lantana..................Rigor.
Larch....................Audacity. Boldness.
Larkspur.................Lightness. Levity.
Larkspur, Pink...........Fickleness.
Larkspur, Purple.........Haughtiness.
Laurel...................Glory.
Laurel, Common, in flower..Perfidy.
Laurel, Ground...........Perseverance.

THE LANGUAGE OF FLOWERS.

Laurel, Mountain ....Ambition.
Laurel-leaved Magnolia..Dignity.
Laurestina...............A token. I die if neglected.
Lavender................Distrust.
Leaves (dead)...........Melancholy.
Lemon...................Zest.
Lemon Blossoms..........Fidelity in love.
Lettuce.................Cold-heartedness.
Lichen..................Dejection. Solitude.
Lilac, Field............Humility.
Lilac, Purple...........First emotions of love.
Lilac, White............Youthful innocence.
Lily, Day...............Coquetry.
Lily, Imperial..........Majesty.
Lily, White.............Purity. Sweetness.
Lily, Yellow............Falsehood. Gaiety.
Lily of the Valley......Return of happiness
Linden or Lime Trees....Conjugal love.
Lint....................I feel my obligation.
Live Oak................Liberty.
Liverwort...............Confidence.
Licorice, Wild..........I declare against you.
Lobelia.................Malevolence.
Locust Tree.............Elegance.
Locust Tree (green).....Affection beyond the grave.
London Pride............Frivolity.
Lote Tree...............Concord.
Lotus...................Eloquence.
Lotus Flower............Estranged love.
Lotus Leaf..............Recantation.
Love in a Mist..........Perplexity.
Love lies Bleeding......Hopeless, not heartless.
Lucern..................Life.
Lupine..................Voraciousness. Imagination.

Madder..................Calumny.
Magnolia................Love of nature.
Magnolia, Swamp.........Perseverance.
Mallow..................Mildness.
Mallow, Marsh...........Beneficence.
Mallow, Syrian..........Consumed by love.
Mallow, Venetian........Delicate beauty.
Manchineal Tree.........Falsehood.
Mandrake................Horror.
Maple...................Reserve.
Marigold................Grief.
Marigold, African.......Vulgar minds.
Marigold, French........Jealousy.
Marigold, Prophetic.....Prediction.
Marigold and Cypress....Despair.
Marjoram................Blushes.
Marvel of Peru..........Timidity.
Meadow Lychnis..........Wit.
Meadow Saffron..........My best days are past.
Meadowsweet.............Uselessness.
Mercury.................Goodness.
Mesembryanthemum........Idleness.
Mezereon................Desire to please.
Michaelmas Daisy........Afterthought.
Mignionette.............Your qualities surpass your charms.
Milfoil.................War.
Milkvetch...............Your presence softens my pains.
Milkwort................Hermitage.

Mimosa (Sensitive Plant).Sensitiveness.
Mint....................Virtue.
Mistletoe...............I surmount difficulties.
Mock Orange.............Counterfeit.
Monkshood (Helmet Flower)....Chivalry. Knight-errantry.
Moonwort................Forgetfulness.
Morning Glory...........Affectation.
Moschatel...............Weakness.
Moss....................Maternal love.
Mosses..................Ennui.
Mossy Saxifrage.........Affection.
Motherwort..............Concealed love.
Mountain Ash............Prudence.
Mourning Bride..........Unfortunate attachment. I have lost all.
Mouse-eared Chickweed...Ingenuous simplicity.
Mouse-eared Scorpion Grass....Forget me not.
Moving Plant............Agitation.
Mudwort.................Tranquillity.
Mugwort.................Happiness.
Mulberry Tree (Black)...I shall not survive you.
Mulberry Tree (White)...Wisdom.
Mushroom................Suspicion.
Musk Plant..............Weakness.
Mustard Seed............Indifference.
Myrobalan...............Privation.
Myrrh...................Gladness.
Myrtle..................Love.

Narcissus...............Egotism.
Nasturtium..............Patriotism.
Nettle Burning..........Slander.
Nettle Tree.............Concert.
Night-blooming Cereus...Transient beauty.
Night Convolvulus.......Night.
Nightshade..............Truth.

Oak Leaves..............Bravery.
Oak Tree................Hospitality.
Oak (White).............Independence.
Oats....................The witching soul of music.
Oleander................Beware.
Olive...................Peace.
Orange Blossoms.........Your purity equals your loveliness.
Orange Flowers..........Chastity. Bridal festivities.
Orange Tree.............Generosity.
Orchis..................A Belle.
Osier...................Frankness.
Osmunda.................Dreams.
Ox Eye..................Patience.

Palm....................Victory.
Pansy...................Thoughts.
Parsley.................Festivity.
Pasque Flower...........You have no claims.
Passion Flower..........Religious superstition.
Patience Dock...........Patience.
Pea, Everlasting........An appointed meeting. Lasting pleasure.
Pea, Sweet..............Departure.

Peach...................Your qualities, like your charms, are unequaled.
Peach Blossom...........I am your captive.
Pear....................Affection.
Pear Tree...............Comfort.
Pennyroyal..............Flee away.
Peony...................Shame. Bashfulness.
Peppermint..............Warmth of feeling.
Periwinkle, Blue........Early friendship.
Periwinkle, White.......Pleasures of memory.
Persicaria..............Restoration.
Persimon................Bury me amid Nature's beauties.
Peruvian Heliotrope.....Devotion.
Pheasant's Eye..........Remembrance.
Phlox...................Unanimity.
Pigeon Berry............Indifference.
Pimpernel...............Change. Assignation.
Pine....................Pity.
Pine-apple..............You are perfect.
Pine, Pitch.............Philosophy.
Pine, Spruce............Hope in adversity.
Pink....................Boldness.
Pink, Carnation.........Woman's love.
Pink, Indian, Double....Always lovely.
Pink, Indian, Single....Aversion.
Pink, Mountain..........Aspiring.
Pink, Red, Double.......Pure and ardent love
Pink, Single............Pure love.
Pink, Variegated........Refusal.
Pink, White.............Ingeniousness. Talent.
Plane Tree..............Genius.
Plum, Indian............Privation.
Plum Tree...............Fidelity.
Plum, Wild..............Independence.
Polyanthus..............Pride of riches.
Polyanthus, Crimson.....The heart's mystery
Polyanthus, Lilac.......Confidence.
Pomegranate.............Foolishness.
Pomegranate Flower......Mature elegance.
Poplar, Black...........Courage.
Poplar, White...........Time.
Poppy, Red..............Consolation.
Poppy, Scarlet..........Fantastic extravagance.
Poppy, White............Sleep. My bane. My antidote.
Potato..................Benevolence.
Prickly Pear............Satire.
Pride of China..........Dissension.
Primrose................Early youth.
Primrose, Evening.......Inconstancy.
Primrose, Red...........Unpatronized merit.
Privet..................Prohibition.
Purple, Clover..........Provident.
Pyrus Japonica..........Fairies' fire.

Quaking-Grass...........Agitation.
Quamoclit...............Busybody.
Queen's Rocket..........You are the queen of coquettes. Fashion.
Quince..................Temptation.

Ragged Robin............Wit.
Ranunculus..............You are radiant with charms.

THE LANGUAGE OF FLOWERS.

Ranunculus, Garden......You are rich in attractions.
Ranunculus, Wild.......Ingratitude.
Raspberry...............Remorse.
Ray Grass...............Vice.
Red Catchfly............Youthful love.
Reed....................Complaisance. Music.
Reed, Split.............Indiscretion.
Rhododendron (Rosebay) Danger. Beware.
Rhubarb.................Advice.
Rocket..................Rivalry.
Rose....................Love.
Rose, Austrian..........Thou art all that is lovely.
Rose, Bridal............Happy love.
Rose, Burgundy..........Unconscious beauty
Rose, Cabbage...........Ambassador of love.
Rose, Campion...........Only deserve my love.
Rose, Carolina..........Love is dangerous.
Rose, China.............Beauty always new.
Rose, Christmas.........Tranquilize my anxiety.
Rose, Daily.............Thy smile I aspire to
Rose, Damask............Brilliant complexion
Rose, Deep Red..........Bashful shame.
Rose, Dog...............Pleasure and pain.
Rose, Guelder...........Winter. Age.
Rose, Hundred-leaved....Pride.
Rose, Japan.............Beauty is your only attraction.
Rose, Maiden Blush......If you love me, you will find it out.
Rose, Multiflora........Grace.
Rose, Mundi.............Variety.
Rose, Musk..............Capricious beauty.
Rose, Musk, Cluster.....Charming.
Rose, Single............Simplicity.
Rose, Thornless.........Early attachment.
Rose, Unique............Call me not beautiful
Rose, White.............I am worthy of you.
Rose, White (withered)..Transient impressions.
Rose, Yellow............Decrease of love. Jealousy.
Rose, York and Lancaster War.
Rose, Full-blown, placed over two Buds........Secrecy.
Rose, White and Red together...............Unity.
Roses, Crown of.........Reward of virtue.
Rosebud, Red............Pure and lovely.
Rosebud, White..........Girlhood.
Rosebud, Moss...........Confession of love.
Rosebay (Rhododendron) Beware. Danger.
Rosemary................Remembrance.
Rudbeckia...............Justice.
Rue.....................Disdain.
Rush....................Docility.
Rye Grass...............Changeable disposition.

Saffron.................Beware of excess.
Saffron Crocus..........Mirth.
Saffron, Meadow.........My happiest days are past.
Sage....................Domestic virtue.
Sage, Garden............Esteem.
Sainfoin................Agitation.
St. John's Wort.........Animosity. Superstition.

Sardony.................Irony.
Saxifrage, Mossy........Affection.
Scabious................Unfortunate love.
Scabious, Sweet.........Widowhood.
Scarlet Lychnis.........Sunbeaming eyes.
Schinus.................Religious enthusiasm.
Scotch Fir..............Elevation.
Sensitive Plant.........Sensibility. Delicate feelings.
Senvy...................Indifference.
Shamrock................Light-heartedness.
Snakesfoot..............Horror.
Snapdragon..............Presumption.
Snowball................Bound.
Snowdrop................Hope.
Sorrel..................Affection.
Sorrel, Wild............Wit ill-timed.
Sorrel, Wood............Joy.
Southernwood............Jest. Bantering.
Spanish Jasmine.........Sensuality. [ment.
Spearmint...............Warmth of senti-
Speedwell...............Female fidelity.
Speedwell, Germander....Facility.
Speedwell, Spiked.......Semblance.
Spider Ophrys...........Adroitness.
Spiderwort..............Esteem, not love.
Spiked Willow Herb......Pretension.
Spindle Tree............Your charms are engraven on my heart.
Star of Bethlehem.......Purity.
Starwort................Afterthought. [age.
Starwort, American......Cheerfulness in old
Stock...................Lasting beauty.
Stock, Ten Week.........Promptness.
Stonecrop...............Tranquillity.
Straw, Broken...........Rupture of a contract.
Straw, Whole............Union.
Strawberry Tree.........Esteem and love.
Sumach, Venice..........Splendor. Intellectual excellence.
Sunflower, Dwarf........Adoration.
Sunflower, Tall.........Haughtiness.
Swallow-wort............Cure for heartache.
Sweet Basil.............Good wishes.
Sweetbrier, American....Simplicity.
Sweetbrier, European....I wound to heal.
Sweetbrier, Yellow......Decrease of love.
Sweet Pea...............Delicate pleasures.
Sweet Sultan............Felicity.
Sweet William...........Gallantry.
Sycamore................Curiosity.
Syringa.................Memory.
Syringa, Carolina.......Disappointment.

Tamarisk................Crime.
Tansy (Wild)............I declare war against you.
Teasel..................Misanthropy.
Tendrils of Climbing Plants................Ties.
Thistle, Common.........Austerity.
Thistle, Fuller's.......Misanthropy.
Thistle, Scotch.........Retaliation.
Thorn, Apple............Deceitful charms.
Thorn, Branch of........Severity.
Thrift..................Sympathy.
Throatwort..............Neglected beauty.
Thyme...................Activity.
Tiger Flower............For once may pride befriend me.

Traveler's Joy..........Safety.
Tree of Life............Old age.
Trefoil.................Revenge.
Tremella Nestoc.........Resistance.
Trillium Pictum.........Modest beauty.
Truffle.................Surprise.
Trumpet Flower..........Fame. [ures.
Tuberose................Dangerous pleas
Tulip...................Fame.
Tulip, Red..............Declaration of love.
Tulip, Variegated.......Beautiful eyes.
Tulip, Yellow...........Hopeless love.
Turnip..................Charity. [you.
Tussilage (Sweet-scented) Justice shall be done
Valerian................An accommodating disposition.
Valerian, Greek.........Rupture.
Venice Sumach...........Intellectual excellence. Splendor.
Venus's Car.............Fly with me.
Venus's Looking-glass...Flattery.
Venus's Trap............Deceit.
Vernal Grass............Poor, but happy.
Veronica................Fidelity.
Vervain.................Enchantment.
Vine....................Intoxication.
Violet, Blue............Faithfulness.
Violet, Dane............Watchfulness.
Violet, Sweet...........Modesty.
Violet, Yellow..........Rural happiness.
Virginian Spiderwort....Momentary happiness.
Virgin's Bower..........Filial love.
Volkamenia..............May you be happy.

Walnut..................Intellect. Stratagem
Wall-flower.............Fidelity in adversity
Water Lily..............Purity of heart.
Water Melon.............Bulkiness.
Wax Plant...............Susceptibility.
Wheat Stalk.............Riches.
Whin....................Anger.
White Jasmine...........Amiableness.
White Lily..............Purity and modesty.
White Mullein...........Good nature.
White Oak...............Independence.
White Pink..............Talent.
White Poplar............Time.
White Rose (dried)......Death preferable to loss of innocence.
Wortleberry.............Treason.
Willow, Creeping........Love forsaken.
Willow, Water...........Freedom.
Willow, Weeping.........Mourning.
Willow-Herb.............Pretension. [ity.
Willow, French..........Bravery and human
Winter Cherry...........Deception.
Witch Hazel.............A spell.
Woodbine................Fraternal love.
Wood Sorrel.............Joy. Maternal tenderness.
Wormwood................Absence.

Xanthium................Rudeness. Pertinacity.
Xeranthemum.............Cheerfulness under adversity.

Yew.....................Sorrow.

Zephyr Flower...........Expectation.
Zinnia..................Thoughts of absent friends.

The Royal Road to the Language of Flowers.

A.

Absence................Wormwood.
Abuse not..............Crocus.
Acknowledgment........Canterbury Bell.
Activity................Thyme.
Admiration.............Amethyst.
Adoration..............Dwarf Sunflower.
Adroitness.............Spider Ophrys.
Adulation..............Cacalia.
Advice................Rhubarb.
Affection..............Mossy Saxifrage.
Affection..............Pear.
Affection..............Sorrel.
Affection beyond the grave. Green Locust.
Affection, maternal.......Cinquefoil.
Affectation............Cockscomb Amaranth.
Affectation............Morning Glory.
Afterthought...........Michaelmas Daisy.
Afterthought...........Starwort.
Afterthought...........China Aster.
Agreement.............Straw.
Age...................Guelder Rose.
Agitation..............Moving Plant.
Agitation..............Sainfoin.
Alas! for my poor heart. Deep Red Carnation
Always cheerful........Coreopsis.
Always lovely..........Indian Pink (double)
Ambassador of love....Cabbage Rose.
Amiability.............Jasmine.
Anger.................Whin.
Animosity.............St. John's Wort.
Anticipation...........Gooseberry.
Anxious and trembling...Red Columbine.
Ardor.................Cuckoo Plant.
Argument..............Fig.
Arts or artifice........Acanthus.
Assiduous to please....Sprig of Ivy with tendrils.
Assignation............Pimpernel.
Attachment............Indian Jasmine.
Audacity...............Larch.
Avarice...............Scarlet Auricula.
Aversion..............China or Indian Pink.

B.

Bantering..............Southernwood.
Baseness..............Dodder of Thyme.
Bashfulness............Peony.
Bashful shame.........Deep Red Rose.
Beautiful eyes.........Variegated Tulip.
Beauty................Party-colored Daisy
Beauty always new.....China Rose.
Beauty, capricious.....Lady's Slipper.
Beauty, capricious.....Musk Rose.
Beauty, delicate.......Flower of an Hour.
Beauty, delicate.......Hibiscus.
Beauty, divine........American Cowslip.
Beauty, glorious.......Glory Flower.
Beauty, lasting........Stock.
Beauty, magnificent....Calla Æthiopica.
Beauty, mental........Clematis.
Beauty, modest.......Trillium Pictum.
Beauty, neglected.....Throatwort.
Beauty, pensive.......Laburnum.
Beauty, rustic.........French Honeysuckle
Beauty, unconscious...Burgundy Rose.
Beauty is your only attraction................Japan Rose.
Belle..................Orchis.
Be mine...............Four-leaved Clover.
Beneficence...........Marshmallow.
Benevolence...........Potato.
Betrayed..............White Catchfly.
Beware................Oleander.
Beware................Rosebay.
Blackness.............Ebony Tree.
Bluntness.............Borage.
Blushes...............Marjoram.
Boaster...............Hydrangea.
Boldness..............Pink.
Bonds.................Convolvulus.
Bonds of affection.....Gillyflower.
Bravery...............Oak Leaves.
Bravery and humanity...French Willow.
Bridal favor...........Ivy Geranium.
Brilliant complexion...Damask Rose.
Bulk..................Water Melon.
Bulk..................Gourd.
Busybody.............Quamoclit.
Bury me amid Nature's beauties..............Persimon.

C.

Call me not beautiful...Rose Unique.
Calm repose..........Buckbean.
Calumny..............Hellebore.
Calumny..............Madder.
Change...............Pimpernel.
Changeable disposition..Rye Grass.
Charity...............Turnip.
Charming.............Cluster of Musk Roses.
Charms deceitful......Thorn Apple.
Cheerfulness in old age..American Starwort.
Cheerfulness under adversity...............Chinese Chrysanthemum.
Chivalry..............Monkshood (Helmet Flower).
Cleanliness...........Hyssop.
Coldheartedness......Lettuce.
Coldness..............Agnus Castus.
Color of my life......Coral Honeysuckle.
Come down...........Jacob's Ladder.
Comfort...............Pear Tree.
Comforting............Scarlet Geranium.
Compassion...........Allspice.
Concealed love.......Motherwort.
Concert...............Nettle Tree.
Concord...............Lote Tree.
Confession of love....Moss Rosebud.
Confidence............Hepatica.
Confidence............Lilac Polyanthus.
Confidence............Liverwort.
Confidence in Heaven..Flowering Reed.
Conjugal love.........Lime, or Linden Tree.
Consolation...........Red Poppy.
Constancy............Bluebell.
Consumed by love....Syrian Mallow.
Counterfeit............Mock Orange.
Courage..............Black Poplar.
Crime.................Tamarisk.
Cure..................Balm of Gilead.
Cure for heartache....Swallow Wort.
Curiosity..............Sycamore.

D.

Danger................Rhododendron. Rosebay.
Dangerous pleasures...Tuberose.
Death.................Cypress.
Death preferable to loss of innocence...........White Rose (dried).
Deceit.................Apocynum.
Deceit.................Flytrap.
Deceit.................Dogsbane.
Deceitful charms......Apple, Thorn.
Deception.............White Cherry Tree.
Declaration of love....Red Tulip.
Decrease of love......Yellow Rose.
Delay.................Eupatorium.
Delicacy..............Bluebottle. Century
Dejection.............Lichen.
Desire to please......Mezereon.
Despair...............Cypress.
Despondency..........Humble Plant.
Devotion..............Peruvian Heliotrope
Difficulty.............Blackthorn.
Dignity...............Cloves.
Dignity...............Laurel-leaved Magnolia.
Disappointment.......Syringa, Carolina.
Disdain...............Yellow Carnation.
Disdain...............Rue.
Disgust...............Frog Ophrys.
Dissension............Pride of China.
Distinction............Cardinal Flower.
Distrust...............Lavender.
Divine beauty.........American Cowslip.
Docility...............Rush.
Domestic industry....Flax.
Domestic virtue.......Sage.
Durability.............Dogwood.
Duration..............Cornel Tree.

E.

Early attachment......Thornless Rose.
Early friendship.......Blue Periwinkle.
Early youth...........Primrose.
Elegance..............Locust Tree.
Elegance and grace...Yellow Jasmine.
Elevation.............Scotch Fir.
Eloquence............Lagerstræmia, Indian.
Enchantment.........Holly Herb.
Enchantment.........Vervain.
Energy in adversity...Camomile.
Envy..................Bramble.
Error..................Bee Ophrys.
Error..................Fly Orchis.
Esteem...............Garden Sage.
Esteem, not love.....Spiderwort.
Esteem and love.....Strawberry Tree.
Estranged love.......Lotus Flower.
Excellence............Camellia Japonica.
Expectation...........Anemone.

THE LANGUAGE OF FLOWERS.

Expectation ....Zephyr Flower.
Expected meeting........Nutmeg Geranium.
Extent ....Gourd.
Extinguished hopes......Major Convolvulus.

F.

Facility ....Germander Speedwell.
Fairies' fire..............Pyrus Japonica.
Faithfulness.............Blue Violet.
Faithfulness ....Heliotrope.
Falsehood ....Bugloss.
Falsehood ....Yellow Lily.
Falsehood ....Manchineal Tree.
Fame....................Tulip. Trumpet Flower.
Fame speaks him great and good...Apple Blossom.
Fantastic extravagance...Scarlet Poppy.
Farewell..................Michaelmas Daisy.
Fascination..............Fern.
Fascination ....Honesty.
Fashion ....Queen's Rocket.
Fecundity................Hollyhock.
Felicity..................Sweet Sultan.
Female fidelity...........Speedwell.
Festivity.................Parsley.
Fickleness ....Abatina.
Fickleness ....Pink Larkspur.
Filial love ....Virgin's bower.
Fidelity ....Veronica. Ivy.
Fidelity ....Plum Tree.
Fidelity in adversity......Wall-flower.
Fidelity in love..........Lemon Blossoms.
Fire ....Fleur-de-Luce.
First emotions of love....Purple Lilac.
Flame ....Fleur-de-lis. Iris.
Flattery ....Venus's Looking-glass.
Flee away................Pennyroyal.
Fly with me..............Venus's Car.
Folly.....................Columbine.
Foppery.................Cockscomb Amaranth.
Foolishness ....Pomegranate.
Foresight................Holly.
Forgetfulness............Moonwort.
Forget me not...........Forget me not.
For once may pride befriend me..............Tiger Flower.
Forsaken ....Garden Anemone.
Forsaken ....Laburnum.
Frankness ....Osier.
Fraternal love ....Woodbine.
Freedom ....Water Willow.
Freshness ....Damask Rose.
Friendship ....Acacia.
Friendship, early........Blue Periwinkle.
Friendship, true.........Oak-leaved Geranium.
Friendship, unchanging..Arbor Vitæ.
Frivolity ....London Pride.
Frugality ....Chicory. Endive.

G.

Gaiety...................Butterfly Orchis.
Gaiety...................Yellow Lily.
Gallantry................Sweet William.
Generosity ....Orange Tree.
Generous and devoted affection............French Honeysuckle.
Genius..................Plane Tree.

Gentility ....Corn Cockle.
Girlhood ....White Rosebud.
Gladness ....Myrrh.
Glory ....Bay Tree.
Glory ....Laurel.
Glorious beauty.........Glory Flower.
Goodness................Bonus Henricus.
Goodness................Mercury.
Good education ....Cherry Tree.
Good wishes............Sweet Basil.
Good nature............White Mullein.
Gossip ....Cobœa.
Grace ....Multiflora Rose.
Grace and elegance.....Yellow Jasmine.
Grandeur...............Ash Tree.
Gratitude ....Small White Bellflower.
Grief ....Harebell.
Grief ....Marigold.

H.

Happy love..............Bridal Rose
Hatred ....Basil.
Haughtiness.............Purple Larkspur.
Haughtiness............Tall Sunflower.
Health..................Iceland Moss.
Hermitage ....Milkwort.
Hidden worth...........Coriander.
Honesty.................Honesty.
Hope ....Flowering Almond.
Hope ....Hawthorn.
Hope ....Snowdrop.
Hope in adversity ......Spruce Pine.
Hopeless love...........Yellow Tulip.
Hopeless, not heartless..Love Lies Bleeding.
Horror..................Mandrake.
Horror..................Dragonswort.
Horror..................Snakesfoot.
Hospitality..............Oak Tree.
Humility ....Broom.
Humility ....Bindweed, Small.
Humility ....Field Lilac.

I.

I am too happy ....Cape Jasmine.
I am your captive.......Peach Blossom.
I am worthy of you.....White Rose.
I change but in death....Bay leaf.
I declare against you....Belvedere.
I declare against you....Licorice.
I declare war against you.Wild Tansy.
I die if neglected.........Laurestina.
I desire a return of affection.................Jonquil.
I feel my obligations.....Lint.
I feel your kindness......Flax.
I have lost all...........Mourning Bride.
I live for thee...........Cedar Leaf.
I love....................Red Chrysanthemum.
I partake of your sentiments................Double China Aster
I partake your sentiments.Garden Daisy.
I shall die to-morrow ....Gum Cistus.
I shall not survive you...Black Mulberry.
I surmount difficulties....Mistletoe.
I will think of it........Single China Aster.
I will think of it.........Wild Daisy.
I wound to heal..........Eglantine (Sweetbrier).
If you love me, you will find it out............Maiden Blush Rose.

Idleness.................Mesembryanthemum.
Ill-natured beauty......Citron.
Imagination ....Lupine.
Immortality............Amaranth (Globe).
Impatience.............Yellow Balsam.
Impatient of absence....Corchorus.
Impatient resolves......Red Balsam.
Imperfection...........Henbane.
Importunity............Burdock.
Inconstancy............Evening Primrose.
Incorruptible ....Cedar of Lebanon.
Independence..........Wild Plum Tree.
Independence..........White Oak.
Indifference...........Candytuft, Everflowering.
Indifference...........Mustard Seed.
Indifference...........Pigeon Berry.
Indifference...........Senvy.
Indiscretion...........Split Reed.
Industry ....Red Clover.
Industry Domestic ....Flax.
Ingeniousness ....White Pink.
Ingenuity.............Penciled Geranium.
Ingenuous Simplicity....Mouse-eared Chickweed.
Ingratitude ....Crowfoot.
Innocence..............Daisy.
Insincerity..............Foxglove.
Insinuation ....Great Bindweed.
Inspiration..............Angelica.
Instability ....Dahlia.
Intellect ....Walnut.
Intoxication ....Vine.
Irony ....Sardony.

J.

Jealousy ....French Marigold.
Jealousy ....Yellow Rose.
Jest......................Southernwood.
Joy ....Wood Sorrel.
Joys to come............Lesser Celandine.
Justice...................Rudbeckia.
Justice shall be done to you ....Coltsfoot.
Justice shall be done to you..................Sweet-scented Tussilage.

K.

Knight-errantry ....Helmet Flower (Monks hood).

L.

Lamentation............Aspen Tree.
Lasting beauty..........Stock.
Lasting pleasures........Everlasting Pea.
Let me go.............:Butterfly Weed.
Levity...... ....Larkspur.
Liberty..................Live Oak.
Life......................Lucern.
Lightheartedness........Shamrock.
Lightness ....Larkspur.
Live for me ....Arbor vitæ.
Love....................Myrtle.
Love....................Rose.
Love, forsaken..........Creeping Willow.
Love returned..........Ambrosia.
Love is dangerous.......Carolina Rose.
Luster...................Aconite-leaved Crowfoot, or Fair Maid of France.
Luxury.................Chestnut Tree.

THE LANGUAGE OF FLOWERS.

M.

Magnificent beauty.......Calla Æthiopica.
Majesty................Crown Imperial.
Malevolence............Lobelia.
Marriage... ....Ivy.
Maternal affection........Cinquefoil.
Maternal love............Moss.
Maternal tenderness......Wood Sorrel
Matrimony...............American Linden.
May you be happy. .....Volkamenia.
Meanness ....Cuscuta.
Meekness ....Birch.
Melancholy ....Dark Geranium.
Melancholy ....Dead Leaves.
Mental beauty...........Clematis.
Mental beauty...........Kennedia.
Message.................Iris.
Mildness.................Mallow.
Mirth ....Saffron Crocus.
Misanthropy............Aconite (Wolfsbane)
Misanthropy ....Fuller's Teasel.
Modest beauty ....Trillium Pictum.
Modest genius...........Creeping Cereus.
Modesty...,............Violet.
Modesty and purity ......White Lily.
Momentary happiness....Virginian Spiderwort.
Mourning................Weeping Willow.
Music...................Bundles of reed, with their panicles
My best days are past.....Colchicum, or Meadow Saffron.
My regrets follow you to the grave.............Asphodel.

N.

Neatness.................Broom.
Neglected beauty........Throatwort.
Never-ceasing remembrance................Everlasting.

O.

Old age ....Tree of Life.
Only deserve my love....Champion Rose.

P.

Painful recollections......Flos Adonis.
Painting..................Auricula.
Painting the lily..........Daphne Odora.
Passion ....White Dittany.
Paternal error............Cardamine.
Patience..................Dock. Ox-eye.
Patriotism................American Elm.
Patriotism................Nasturtium.
Peace ....Olive.
Perfected loveliness......Camellia Japonica, White.
Perfidy...................Common Laurel, in flower.
Pensive beauty ....Laburnum.
Perplexity................Love in a mist.
Persecution ....Checkered Fritillary.
Perseverance............Swamp Magnolia.
Persuasion...............Althea Frutex.
Persuasion...............Syrian Mallow.
Pertinacity...............Clotbur.
Pity.....................Pine.
Pleasure and pain........Dog Rose.
Pleasure, Lasting.........Everlasting Pea.
Pleasures of memory.....White Periwinkle.

Popular favor............Cistust or Rock Rose.
Poverty ....Evergreen Clematis
Power....................Imperial Montague.
Power....................Cress.
Precaution ....Golden Rod.
Prediction ....Prophetic Marigold.
Pretension ....Spiked Willow Herb
Pride....................Amaryllis.
Pride....................Hundred-leaved Rose.
Privation..... ....Indian Plum.
Privation................Myrobalan.
Profit....................Cabbage.
Prohibition..............Privet.
Prolific..................Fig Tree.
Promptness..............Ten-week Stock.
Prosperity...............Beech Tree.
Protection ....Bearded Crepis.
Prudence ....Mountain Ash.
Pure love.. ....Single Red Pink.
Pure and ardent love....Double Red Pink.
Pure and lovely ....Red Rosebud.
Purity...................Star of Bethlehem.

Q.

Quarrel ....Broken Corn-straw.
Quicksightedness........Hawkweed.

R.

Reason..................Goat's Rue.
Recantation.............Lotus Leaf.
Recall...................Silver-leaved Geranium.
Reconciliation...........Filbert.
Reconciliation...........Hazel.
Refusal..................Striped Carnation.
Regard ....Daffodil.
Relief....................Balm of Gilead.
Relieve my anxiety......Christmas Rose.
Religious superstition ....Aloe.
Religious superstition....Passion Flower.
Religious enthusiasm.....Schinus.
Remembrance...........Rosemary.
Remorse................Bramble.
Remorse................Raspberry.
Rendezvous.............Chickweed.
Reserve.................Maple.
Resistance ....Tremella Nestoc.
Restoration.............Persicaria.
Retaliation..............Scotch Thistle.
Return of happiness....Lily of the Valley.
Revenge ....Birdsfoot Trefoil.
Reverie ....Flowering Fern.
Reward of merit........Bay Wreath.
Reward of virtue ....Garland of Roses.
Riches..... ....Corn.
Rigor...... ....Lantana.
Rivalry..................Rocket.
Rudeness...............Clotbur.
Rudeness...............Xanthium.
Rural happiness.........Yellow Violet.
Rustic beauty...........French Honeysuckle
Rustic oracle............Dandelion.

S.

Sadness.................Dead Leaves.
Safety...................Traveler's Joy.
Satire ....Prickly Pear.
Sculpture................Hoya.
Secret love..............Yellow Acacia.
Semblance..............Spiked Speedwell.

Sensitiveness............Mimosa.
Sensuality...............Spanish Jasmine.
Separation...............Carolina Jasmine.
Severity.................Branch of Thorns.
Shame...... ....Peony.
Sharpness..............Barberry Tree.
Sickness................Anemone (Zephyr Flower).
Silliness.................Fool's Parsley.
Simplicity.....,........American Sweetbrier.
Sincerity................Garden Chervil.
Slighted love...........Yellow Chrysanthemum.
Snare...................Catchfly. Dragon Plant.
Solitude.................Heath.
Sorrow..................Yew.
Sourness of temper......Barberry.
Spell....................Circæa.
Spleen..................Fumitory.
Splendid beauty.........Amaryllis.
Splendor................Austurtium.
Sporting................Fox-tail Grass.
Steadfast piety..........Wild Geranium.
Stoicism ....Box Tree.
Strength................Cedar. Fennel.
Submission.............Grass.
Submission.............Harebell.
Success crown your wishes..............Coronella.
Succor..................Juniper.
Sunbeaming eyes........Scarlet Lychnis.
Surprise.................Truffle.
Susceptibility ....Wax Plant.
Suspicion...............Champignon.
Sympathy .,...........Balm.
Sympathy..............Thrift.

T.

Talent ....White Pink.
Tardiness ....Flax-leaved Goldylocks.
Taste ....Scarlet Fuschia.
Tears ....Helenium.
Temperance ....Azalea.
Temptation ....Apple.
Thankfulness ....Agrimony.
The color of my fate .....Coral Honeysuckle.
The heart's mystery......Crimson Polyanthus
The perfection of female loveliness ....Justicia.
The witching soul of music ....Oats.
Thoughts ....Pansy.
Thoughts of absent friends................Zinnia.
Thy frown will kill me...Currant.
Thy smile I aspire to.....Daily Rose.
Ties....................Tendrils of Climbing Plants.
Timidity ....Amaryllis.
Timidity ....Marvel of Peru.
Time................. ..White Poplar.
Tranquillity.............Mudwort.
Tranquillity.............Stonecrop.
Tranquilize my anxiety...Christmas Rose.
Transient beauty........Night-blooming Cereus.
Transient impressions....Withered White Rose.
Transport of joy.........Cape Jasmine.

THE LANGUAGE OF FLOWERS.

Treachery.. ....Bilberry.
True love ....Forget me not.
True friendship.........Oak-leaved Geranium.
Truth ....Bitter sweet Nightshade.
Truth ....White Chrysanthemum.

U.
Unanimity ....Phlox.
Unbelief.................Judas Tree.
Unceasing remembrance.American Cudweed
Unchanging friendship...Arbor Vitæ.
Unconscious beauty......Burgundy Rose.
Unexpected meeting.....Lemon Geranium.
Unfortunate attachment..Mourning Bride.
Unfortunate love.........Scabious.
Union....................Whole Straw.
Unity ....White and Red Rose together.
Unpatronized merit......Red Primrose.
Uselessness ....Meadowsweet.
Utility ....Grass.

V.
Variety ....China Aster.
Variety ....Mundi Rose.
Vice ....Darnel (Ray Grass).
Victory ....Palm.
Virtue ....Mint.
Virtue, Domestic.........Sage.
Volubility...............Abecedary.
Voraciousness...........Lupine.
Vulgar minds............African Marigold.

W.
War.....................York and Lancaster Rose.
War ....Achillea Millefolia.
Warlike trophy..........Indian Cress.
Warmth of feeling ......Peppermint.
Watchfulness............Dame Violet.
Weakness...............Moschatel.
Weakness ....Musk Plant.
Welcome to a stranger ..American Starwort
Widowhood ....Sweet Scabious.
Win me and wear me ....Lady's Slipper.
Winning grace..........Cowslip.
Winter..................Guelder Rose.
Wit. ....Meadow Lychnis.
Wit ill-timed............Wild Sorrel.
Witchcraft ....Enchanter's Nightshade.
Worth beyond beauty....Sweet Alyssum.
Worth sustained by judicious and tender affection...................Pink Convolvulus.
Worthy all praise........Fennel.

Y.
You are cold ....Hortensia.
You are my divinity......American Cowslip.
You are perfect..........Pine Apple.
You are radiant with charms................Ranunculus.
You are rich in attractions Garden Ranunculus
You are the queen of coquettes................Queen's Rocket.
You have no claims .....Pasque Flower.
You please all...........Branch of Currants.
You will be my death ....Hemlock.
Your charms are engraven on my heart ....Spindle Tree.
Your looks freeze me.....Ice Plant.
Your presence softens my pains..................Milkvetch.
Your purity equals your loveliness ....Orange Blossoms.
Your qualities, like your charms, are unequaled..Peach.
Your qualities surpass your charms...........Mignionette.
Youthful innocence.......White Lilac.
Youthful love............Red Catchfly.

Z.
Zealousness ....Elder.
Zest ....Lemon

TREASURES OF THE PAST FROM TRIDAC PUBLISHING

VICTORIAN PARLOR GAMES AND ACTIVITIES

EDWARDIAN FASHION IN PHOTOGRAPHS

PALACES OF SIN, OR, THE DEVIL IN SOCIETY (1902)

VICTORIAN FASHION NOTEBOOK

THE BLOOD SACRIFICE COMPLEX: HUMAN SACRIFICE, CANNIBALISM, AND CIRCUMCISION FROM A GLOBAL PERSPECTIVE

For information on new releases, please visit

tridacpublishing.com

Made in the USA
Monee, IL
06 July 2023